Laura Doernbach
Patrick Büttner

Englisch

KOOPERATIV!

Klasse 7

Kernthemen des Lehrplans
mit kooperativen Lernmethoden
erfolgreich umsetzen

Auer

Gedruckt auf umweltbewusst gefertigtem, chlorfrei gebleichtem und alterungsbeständigem Papier.

1. Auflage 2016
Nach den seit 2006 amtlich gültigen Regelungen der Rechtschreibung

Umschlaggrafik: © Kritina Afanasyeva – Fotolia, © alexghidan89 – Fotolia
Illustrationen: Corina Beurenmeister, Julia Flasche, Carmen Hochmann, Steffen Jähde, Stefan Lohr, Thorsten Trantow, Georg Wieborg
Satz: fotosatz griesheim GmbH
Druck und Bindung: Korrekt Nyomdaipari Kft.
ISBN 978-3-403-**07792**-3
www.auer-verlag.de

Was ist kooperatives Lernen?

Beim kooperativen Lernen arbeiten die Schüler[1] als gleichberechtigte Lernpartner in Kleingruppen zusammen. Dabei werden kognitives und soziales Lernen miteinander verbunden: Neben den Lerninhalten kommt den sozialen Prozessen eine besondere Bedeutung zu – die Gruppenmitglieder entwickeln eine positive gegenseitige Abhängigkeit in dem Wissen, dass sie nur als wirkliches Team erfolgreich sein können. In der Kooperation nehmen die Schüler abwechselnd die Rolle eines Lehrenden und die eines Lernenden ein.

Kooperative Arbeitsformen im Unterricht

Kooperatives Lernen stellt eine große Bereicherung für den Unterricht dar: Im Austausch mit anderen erreichen die Schüler ein tieferes Verständnis der Inhalte; sie argumentieren, sie entwickeln und reflektieren Begriffe und Vorgehensweisen, sie vergleichen unterschiedliche Lösungswege und verwenden verschiedene Darstellungsebenen für die Präsentation ihrer Ergebnisse. Wissen wird auf diese Weise flexibler und vom Kontext unabhängiger. Langfristig erlernen die Schüler beim kooperativen Arbeiten die grundlegenden sozialen Kompetenzen, um auch im Team erfolgreich zu arbeiten: sich abzusprechen, sich zu akzeptieren und miteinander zu kooperieren. Fachliches und soziales Lernen werden gleichermaßen gefördert – was auch im zukünftigen Arbeitsleben eine besondere Bedeutung hat.

Weitere Effekte kooperativen Lernens

- Die Schüler entwickeln eine positive Einstellung zum Lerngegenstand.
- Das soziale Klima in der Klasse verbessert sich.
- Die Fähigkeit zum selbstständigen Arbeiten wird auf- und ausgebaut.
- Die Kommunikations- und Kooperationsfähigkeit steigt.
- Das Selbstwertgefühl und die Bereitschaft zur Verantwortungsübernahme steigen an.
- Lernen wird umso effektiver, je aktiver die Schüler bei der Informationsaufnahme tätig sind. Individuelle Lernstrategien können entwickelt und ausprobiert werden. Neue Informationen müssen mit vorhandenen Informationen in Verbindung gesetzt werden.

Die Reihe „Englisch kooperativ"

Kooperative Arbeitsformen werden im Unterricht häufig aus pragmatischen Gründen vernachlässigt: Es herrscht Unsicherheit bei der Umsetzung der Lernmethoden; der Aufwand für das Erstellen eigener Materialien ist hoch. Die Aufgabenstellungen müssen so angelegt sein, dass Kooperation sinnvoll wird und die Schüler durch das Zusammenarbeiten für ihr Lernen profitieren.
Die Reihe „Englisch kooperativ" geht genau diese Probleme an und bietet Abhilfe: praxiserprobte Materialien zum schnellen Unterrichtseinsatz mit Hinweisen, wie der Einsatz der Methoden erfolgreich funktioniert. Dabei werden Kernthemen des Lehrplans abgedeckt, die sich optimal für kooperatives Lernen eignen. Die Bände der einzelnen Jahrgangsstufen bauen aufeinander auf: Bereits verwendete Methoden, mit denen die Schüler schon sicher umgehen können, werden wieder aufgegriffen und mit neuen Methoden kombiniert.

Zur Arbeit mit dem Band

Jedes Thema wird mit einer oder mehreren kooperativen Arbeitsform(en) verknüpft. Die Themen können Einzelstunden oder auch Teil einer Sequenz sein. Im Rahmen jeder Einheit erfolgen zunächst kurze und kompakt dargestellte Hinweise für die Lehrkraft. An dieser Stelle wird kurz auf die kooperative Lernmethode eingegangen und erläutert, wie und warum sich diese Methode besonders für die Thematik eignet. Danach werden fachdidaktische Anmerkungen, Tipps und Hinweise zur Durchführung gegeben. Zusätzlich wird das benötigte Material aufgelistet. Die entsprechenden Kopiervorlagen werden direkt mitgeliefert. So kann fachlich fundiert, aber trotzdem ganz unkompliziert eine Einheit mit kooperativem Lernen umgesetzt werden.
Die im Band verwendeten Methoden werden am Ende des Buches nochmals in kompakten Methodensteckbriefen erklärt und veranschaulicht. Lösungen zu den Arbeitsmaterialien runden den Band ab.

Mit diesen Materialien schaffen Sie erfolgreich eine kooperative Lernkultur, die zum Lernerfolg Ihrer Schüler beiträgt – gerade auch in heterogenen Klassen.

Viel Freude und Erfolg dabei wünschen Ihnen
Laura Doernbach und Patrick Büttner

[1] Aufgrund der besseren Lesbarkeit ist in diesem Buch mit Schüler auch immer Schülerin gemeint, ebenso verhält es sich mit Lehrer und Lehrerin etc.

Methode

In Gruppen bearbeiten die Schüler unterschiedliche Aufgaben. Anschließend erstellt jede Gruppe zu ihrem Thema eine Mindmap, die auf dem Tisch ausgelegt wird. Jeder Schüler innerhalb der Gruppe erhält eine Nummer. Ein Gruppenmitglied bleibt an seinem Tisch. Die anderen Schüler verteilen sich so auf die Tische, dass alle, die die gleiche Nummer erhalten haben, vor der gleichen Mindmap stehen. Der „Experte“, der am jeweiligen Thema gearbeitet hat, fasst nun für seine Mitschüler die wichtigsten Informationen zusammen. Diese machen sich Notizen.
Nach einem Signal des Lehrers wechseln alle Gruppen an einen neuen Tisch und der Schüler, der an der Erstellung des nächsten Produktes beteiligt war, erklärt dieses usw. Die Exhibition ist beendet, wenn alle Sehenswürdigkeiten vorgestellt wurden.

Hinweise/Tipps

Die Schüler werden in fünf Gruppen aufgeteilt und bearbeiten gemeinsam innerhalb ihrer Gruppe jeweils einen Text einer Sehenswürdigkeit. Nach dem Lesen des Textes soll in jeder Gruppe ein Austausch stattfinden, um sicherzustellen, dass der Text von allen Gruppenmitgliedern verstanden wurde. Erst danach soll jeder Schüler die wichtigsten Informationen anhand von Stichpunkten festhalten. Anschließend erstellen sie gemeinsam eine Mindmap zu der jeweiligen Sehenswürdigkeit.
Der Lehrer hat während der Exhibition zweimal die Möglichkeit, Einfluss auf die Gruppenzusammenstellungen zu nehmen. Ob Zufallsgruppen oder leistungsdifferenzierte Gruppen besser geeignet sind, sollte je nach Klasse entschieden werden. Es bietet sich jedoch gerade in der ersten Austauschphase, in der das Textverständnis und das Notieren von Stichpunkten im Vordergrund stehen, an, schwächeren Schülern eine Orientierung an leistungsstärkeren Schülern zu ermöglichen.
Alternativ können die Produkte für die zweite Austauschphase auch an unterschiedliche Wandseiten gehängt werden und die Präsentationen finden im Stehen statt.
Je nachdem, wie viel Zeit zur Verfügung steht, bietet es sich nach der Exhibition an, dass die Schüler wieder in ihre Stammgruppe zurückkehren und ihre Aufzeichnungen der unterschiedlichen Präsentationen vergleichen.
Andere Möglichkeiten, das Text- und Hörverständnis sicherzustellen, wären ein Quiz, bei dem der Lehrer Fragen zu den verschiedenen Sehenswürdigkeiten stellt, oder ein Lückentext.
Die Schüler können sich hierbei durch Fragen bei der jeweiligen Expertengruppe nochmals rückversichern.

Material

- Materialseite 1 in Klassenstärke
- Materialseiten 2 bis 6: je ein Text pro Gruppenmitglied
- Materialseite 7 in doppelter Klassenstärke
- bunte Stifte
- eventuell Bilder der Sehenswürdigkeiten

1 **a** Create an acrostic. Find a London sight for each letter.

L
O
N
D
O
N

S
I
G
H
T
S

b Which sights are hidden in the wordsnakes? Colour them and write them in the list below. Watch the spelling.

2 GROUP A

a Read the text and mark the most important information.

b Talk to your group and discuss what you've marked.

c Write short notes in your exercise book.

d Design a mind map with your group about Tower Bridge.

Tower Bridge

Tower Bridge is one of the most beautiful and most impressive bridges of the world. It was built in 1894 and is about 244 metres long. About 40,000 people cross Tower Bridge every day. You can get across the bridge by car or bus or you can walk and enjoy a beautiful view. People who walk use the pedestrian (= *Fußgänger*) bridge. It has windows so that visitors can take pictures. You can also look at pictures and videos about the history and the design of Tower Bridge. It's interesting to watch a big ship going by. Then all the traffic on the bridge stops because the two parts of the bridge open up to let the ship go through. The bridge needs 90 seconds to lift. Don't be afraid to walk on the pedestrian bridge while the two parts of Tower Bridge open up – the pedestrian bridge doesn't open.

2 GROUP B

a Read the text and mark the most important information.

b Talk to your group and discuss what you've marked.

c Write short notes in your exercise book.

d Design a mind map with your group about Buckingham Palace.

Buckingham Palace

Buckingham Palace is one of the world's most famous buildings and a big tourist attraction in London: more than 50,000 people visit the palace every year. The Queen and the Royal Family live there. The palace has about 600 rooms, a swimming pool, a cinema and also a really big garden with a lot of trees around it. The Queen has a garden party there every summer. In August and September the doors are open to every tourist. You always know when the Queen is there: look at the flag on top of the palace. If you can see the flag, the Queen is at home.

2 GROUP C

a Read the text and mark the most important information.

b Talk to your group and discuss what you've marked.

c Write short notes in your exercise book.

d Design a mind map with your group about Madame Tussauds.

Madame Tussauds

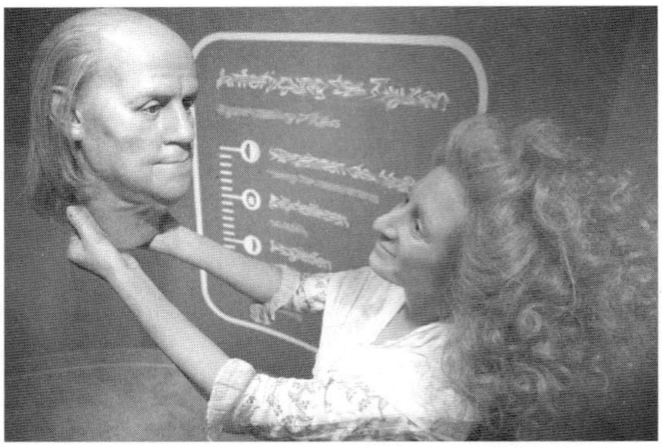

Madame Tussauds is a wax museum with famous people from the areas of entertainment, sports and politics. There are no bodyguards, you can get as close as you want to the stars. One of the main attractions of the museum is the Chamber of Horrors. This part of the museum includes some victims (= *Opfer*) of the French Revolution and also newly-created figures of murderers and other criminals. The wax museum has now become a major tourist attraction in London. It has expanded (= *sich ausbreiten*) with branches (= *Ableger*) in Amsterdam, Las Vegas, New York City, Hong Kong, Shanghai, Washington D.C., Berlin and Hollywood. The museum is named after its founder, Madame Tussaud. She was born in France where she learnt how to make waxworks. In 1802, she came to England with her collection and travelled around Great Britain and Ireland. In 1835, she finally opened a wax exhibition (= *Ausstellung*) in London. Her last work was her self-portrait, which is at the entrance of the museum. Madame Tussaud was 89 years old when she died in 1850.

---

2 GROUP D

a Read the text and mark the most important information.

b Talk to your group and discuss what you've marked.

c Write short notes in your exercise book.

d Design a mind map with your group about Brick Lane Market.

Brick Lane Market

Brick Lane is one of London's most popular tourist attractions. There are a lot of great markets in London, but Brick Lane Market is the biggest. It's near Tower Hamlets. Lots of young people go there to look for trendy second-hand clothes. You can find almost everything there: from cheap leather clothes to stylish furniture. Brick Lane is full of interesting shops and great Indian restaurants, too. The best day to visit Brick Lane is on Sundays, but the shops and restaurants are open every day. You also see street performers (= *Straßenkünstler*) and musicians on every corner. The nearest Tube station is Aldgate East (about seven minutes away on foot).

2 GROUP E

a Read the text and mark the most important information.

b Talk to your group and discuss what you've marked.

c Write short notes in your exercise book.

d Design a mind map with your group about the London Eye.

London Eye

The London Eye is about 135 metres high and one of the biggest Ferris wheels in the world. You can find it on the River Thames, opposite Big Ben. Each high-tech glass capsule can carry 25 people. So in one day, the 32 capsules of the wheel can carry over 15,000 visitors. The London Eye is the UK's most popular tourist attraction and more than 3.5 million people visit it every year. A ride on the London Eye takes about 30 minutes. From up there you have a fantastic view over London. You can see the Houses of Parliament, Buckingham Palace and St. Paul's Cathedral. On a clear day you can see almost 40 kilometres in each direction. The London Eye was built in 2000 to celebrate (= *feiern*) the new millennium (= *Jahrtausend*). It was created (= *entworfen*) by David Marks and Julia Barfield, a married architect team. The main sponsor of the London Eye was the company "British Airways".

2 GROUP F

a Read the text and mark the most important information.

b Talk to your group and discuss what you've marked.

c Write short notes in your exercise book.

d Design a mind map with your group about Hyde Park.

Hyde Park

Hyde Park was created (= *erschaffen*) in 1536 by Henry VIII for hunting. It's one of the royal parks, which means it belongs to the Queen. Hyde Park is nice and green and you can see more than 4,000 trees. There is something for everyone in Hyde Park: you can relax, walk or play ball games. There is also a big lake (Serpentine Lake) where you can paddle with a boat. The park is divided in two (= *zweigeteilt*) by the Serpentine and the Long Water. Many people have a picnic in the park. It's easy to forget that you are in the middle of London. In the evening you can go to open air concerts. The most famous and most crowded (= *überfüllt*) concert in Hyde Park was *The Rolling Stones* in 1969 with about 250,000 to 500,000 visitors. The park is open from 5 am until midnight.

2 GROUP G

a Read the text and mark the most important information.

b Talk to your group and discuss what you've marked.

c Write short notes in your exercise book.

d Design a mind map with your group about the London Dungeon.

London Dungeon

The London Dungeon is in an old prison under the ground. Today, it's a tourist attraction near London Bridge railway station. In the museum you can take a journey through England's brutal history. There are actors who show how life was in the past. There you can take fun rides (= *mit Fahrgeschäften fahren*), see special effects and wax figures. It opened in 1976 and was a museum of "horrible history". It has become so popular, that it's more an entertainment museum now. However, you must be careful: you can get lost in a labyrinth where actors jump out of corners to scare you. Some other scenes of London's brutal history which you can see in the London Dungeon are: The Great Plague (= *Pest*) of London, The Great Fire of London and Jack the Ripper.

---

2 GROUP H

a Read the text and mark the most important information.

b Talk to your group and discuss what you've marked.

c Write short notes in your exercise book.

d Design a mind map with your group about the Trocadero.

The Trocadero

The London Trocadero is a big and famous shopping and entertainment centre near Piccadilly Circus. It covers an area of about 46,450m². It was only a restaurant when it opened in 1846. Today it is a tourist place where you can meet, shop, eat and have fun. In the Trocadero there are lots of restaurants, bars and shops. If you go there, make sure you have enough pocket money. Funland is also a famous place at the London Trocadero. It's one of London's largest entertainment places. There you can find the newest high-tech video games and virtual reality simulators. You can play for hours and hours. They also have lots of assistants who will help you if you have trouble with one of the machines.

2 GROUP I

a Read the text and mark the most important information.

b Talk to your group and discuss what you've marked.

c Write short notes in your exercise book.

d Design a mind map with your group about the Natural History Museum.

Natural History Museum

The Natural History museum is one of London's most popular tourist attractions. It first opened its doors in 1881 and today about five million people visit it every year. You can go in for free and look around all day. There you can find out a lot about plants, animals, insects and even dinosaurs. Best of all is the Earthquake Room. If you would like to be in the middle of an earthquake, this is the place to go. The museum shops are a great place to buy souvenirs or a present for the family. The museum opens at 10 am and closes at 6 pm. More than 300 scientists (= *Wissenschaftler*) work in the museum.

---

2 GROUP J

a Read the text and mark the most important information.

b Talk to your group and discuss what you've marked.

c Write short notes in your exercise book.

d Design a mind map with your group about Piccadilly Circus.

Piccadilly Circus

Piccadilly Circus is the centre of London's nightlife. Its neon lights are famous all over the world. It's a popular crossing and a public square (= *Platz*). Piccadilly Circus was built in 1819 to connect Regent Street with Piccadilly Street. Today, it's a famous meeting point and a tourist attraction. The video display and the neon lights on the corner building on the northern side are well-known. At Piccadilly Circus you can also find the famous Eros fountain, which is a great meeting point. You can meet your friends there if you want to go to one of the restaurants, bars, nightclubs or theatres.
At Piccadilly Circus there is also the new Madame Tussauds's Rock Circus with wax figures of famous rock stars. Rock Circus tells you the story of rock and pop music from the 1950s until today. At the entrance (= *Eingang*) of the museum you get headphones, so you can hear the stars sing. The highlight of the museum is a great concert with wax figures which can move.

3 Your teacher will give you a number. Form a group with all the pupils that have got the same number. One member of another group will present his/her tourist attraction. Use this chart to take notes.

Checklist

name of the tourist attraction					
what it is					
what it looks like					
how old it is					
where it is					
what you can see/do there					
what is special about it					
further information					

Methode

Mit einem Partner beschäftigen sich die Schüler mit den vorgegebenen Materialien. In dieser Phase arbeiten sie gemeinsam an Übungen und können sich bei Unklarheiten in einem geschützten Raum gegenseitig helfen. Nach der Bearbeitung ihrer Aufgaben erstellen die Paare eigene Übungen und Rätsel, die in der nächsten Phase mit einem weiteren Partnerpaar ausgetauscht werden.

Hinweise/Tipps

In der ersten Partnerarbeitsphase beschäftigen sich die Schüler intensiv mit der englischen Fragestellung. Sie besprechen sich mit ihrem Lernpartner und tauschen Ideen für mögliche Rätsel aus, die sie selbst erstellen. Es bietet sich hierbei an, die Schüler darauf hinzuweisen, dass die von ihnen entworfenen Aufgaben anschließend von einem anderen Partnerpaar bearbeitet werden sollen. Daher sollten sie sauber und ordentlich arbeiten und eine Lösungsseite erstellen.
Entweder kann der Lehrer die Partnerkonstellationen im Vorhinein bestimmen oder ähnlich verfahren wie bei der Methode Lerntempoduett: Sobald ein Partnerpaar mit den gesamten Aufgaben fertig ist, steht es auf und positioniert sich für andere sichtbar an einer vorher abgesprochenen Stelle im Klassenraum, um zu signalisieren, dass es fertig ist. Das nächste Paar, das seine Arbeit beendet hat, holt es ab. Zu viert suchen sie sich einen freien Platz im Klassenraum und arbeiten gemeinsam weiter, indem sie ihre erstellten Rätsel austauschen, bearbeiten und anschließend besprechen.

Material

- Materialseiten 1 bis 3 in Klassenstärke

Asking questions

1 **a** Match the correct translation. Write down the answer in the following chart.

a	b	c	d	e	f	g	h	i	j	k	l	m	n	o	p	q	r	s	t	u	v	w	x	y	z

a) Wie geht es dir?

b) Wer hat das gesagt?

c) Kennst du den Weg?

d) Können Sie mir helfen?

e) Ist es weit?

f) In welchem Hotel übernachtest du?

g) Was ist das?

h) Mag dein Vater das Museum?

i) Warum möchtest du nicht den Bus nehmen?

j) Wer singt im Hyde Park?

k) Wann fängt das Konzert an?

l) Wie ist deine Adresse?

m) Wann fängt die Führung an?

n) Wie lange bleibst du in London?

o) Woher kommst du?

p) Wo ist die nächste U-Bahn-Haltestelle?

q) Ist der Buckingham Palace deine Lieblingssehenswürdigkeit in London?

r) Um wie viel Uhr fährt der Bus?

s) Warst du schon mal in London?

t) Warum möchtest du nochmal zu Madame Tussauds gehen?

u) Bist du müde?

v) Ist dein Bruder im Museum?

w) Wo treffen wir uns wieder?

x) Kannst du meinen Kaffee bezahlen?

y) Wer möchte nochmal mit dem London Eye fahren?

z) Wie hoch ist das London Eye?

1. Why don't you want to take the bus?
2. Do you know the way?
3. How long are you going to stay in London?
4. Can you help me?
5. When does the concert start?
6. Is it far?
7. Where are you from?
8. Does your father like the museum?
9. What is that?
10. Who said that?

11. Where is the next underground station?

12. What hotel are you staying at?

13. Is Buckingham Palace your favourite sight in London?

14. Who sings in Hyde Park?

15. How are you?

16. What's your address?

17. When does the guided tour start?

18. Is your brother at the museum?

19. Where do we meet again?

20. Can you pay for my coffee?

21. Who wants to ride the London Eye again?

22. Have you ever been to London before?

23. What time does the bus depart?

24. How high is the London Eye?

25. Why do you want to go to Madame Tussauds again?

26. Are you tired?

b Take a sheet of paper. Create an exercise with a partner like 1a.

2 **a** Find the questions to the following answers.

1. ______________________________ – I'm Jana.
2. ______________________________ – I'm 14 years old.
3. ______________________________ – I'm 1.60 metres.
4. ______________________________ – My address is Bahnhofstraße 15.
5. ______________________________ – I'm from Munich.
6. ______________________________ – My favourite actor is Till Schweiger.
7. ______________________________ – I collect models and I play football.
8. ______________________________ – My hair colour is blond.
9. ______________________________ – My eye colour is brown.
10. ______________________________ – I like cats.
11. ______________________________ – I don't like mice and rats.
12. ______________________________ – I can play the piano well.

b Take a sheet of paper. Create an exercise with a partner like 2a.

3 **a** Complete the mind map by writing questions about the sentence in the middle. Examples: Who is Paul's best friend? Why is the house green? When is Paul's birthday?

Who ____________________
____________________?

Why ____________________
____________________?

Paul lives in a green house near Buckingham Palace.

What ____________________
____________________?

When ____________________
____________________?

Where ____________________
____________________?

b Can you find more questions? You can also start the questions with *Is, Does* or *Has.* Try to find as many questions as possible and write them in your exercise book.
Examples: *Is* Paul tall? *Does* Paul like chocolate? *Has* Paul got a pet?

c Create similar exercises with a partner. Think of a sentence and write it in the middle of a mind map. Give some examples of possible questions.

d You can also make a competition: who can find more questions? You can play with a partner or a group.

4 **a** Write a dialogue in English. Use the following instructions.

A: Bitte höflich um Hilfe.

B: Frage, wie du helfen kannst.

A: Du erzählst, dass du dich verlaufen hast und die Jugendherberge suchst.

B: Versichere, dass es nicht weit von hier ist. Beschreibe, dass er an der Ampel rechts abbiegen muss. Er kann es nicht verfehlen.

A: Bedanke dich.

B: Reagiere darauf und wünsche noch einen schönen Tag.

A: Wünsche ebenfalls einen schönen Tag.

b Practice the dialogue with your partner.

c Create a similar dialogue with your partner. Can you find more questions for a friendly dialogue?

Methode

Die Schüler beschäftigen sich anhand der vorbereiteten Materialien auf zwei verschiedene Arten mit Rollenspielen: Sie präsentieren ein vorgegebenes Gespräch und sie überarbeiten ein Gespräch und setzen es innerhalb einer Partnerarbeit um.
Das Rollenspiel bietet sich bei diesem Thema an, da die Schüler in Partnerarbeit in unterschiedliche Rollen schlüpfen und so auf spielerische Art und Weise Dialogstrukturen einüben können.
Da die Materialien zum Teil in Partnerarbeit zu bearbeiten sind, werden die Lernenden in ihrer kommunikativen und sozialen Kompetenz gefördert.

Hinweise/Tipps

Die Schüler beschäftigen sich zunächst sehr intensiv mit Frage- und Satzstrukturen einer U-Bahn-Wegbeschreibung. Es empfiehlt sich, den Schülern (wenn vorhanden) einen echten U-Bahn-Plan auszuhändigen oder alternativ den U-Bahn-Plan im Englischbuch zu benutzen. Zudem wäre eine Farbkopie des U-Bahn-Plans denkbar. Während der Übungen sollen die Schüler weitere Möglichkeiten der Wegbeschreibung kennenlernen und auf ihren eigenen Dialog anwenden.
Es ist empfehlenswert, die Schüler auf mögliche Requisiten hinzuweisen. Durch Requisiten fällt es vielen Schülern leichter, in eine andere Rolle zu schlüpfen bzw. eine erfundene Situation darzustellen.

Material

- Materialseiten 1 bis 3 in Klassenstärke
- Londoner U-Bahn-Plan, evtl. im Schulbuch
- eigene Requisiten für die Dialoge

The London Underground

1 a Look at the words in the box and match them to the given categories in the table. Use a map of the London Underground for help.

Piccadilly Circus Bakerloo get on southbound
Travelcard Central Chancery Lane Moorgate
northbound Circle change to District
Temple Hammersmith & City Queensway get off
Jubilee Metropolitan westbound Paddington
rush hour Temple zone Northern Piccadilly
Waterloo & City Victoria eastbound Angel platform

underground lines	stations	verbs	other words (adjectives, nouns, ...)

b Can you think of more words? Add them to the table.

2 **a** You are at Oxford Circus. Use your Tube map and try to describe the way to the following sights. Write short notes in the boxes. The example might help you.

Example:

Sight: **Big Ben**
Tube station: Westminster
Line(s):
– Victoria Line southbound
– get off at Victoria
– change to Circle Line or District Line eastbound

Sight: **Buckingham Palace**
Tube station: St. James's Park
Line(s): ______

Sight: **The Trocadero**
Tube station: Piccadilly Circus
Line(s): ______

Sight: **Natural History Museum**
Tube station: South Kensington
Line(s): ______

Sight: **Madame Tussauds**
Tube station: Baker Street
Line(s): ______

Sight:	**The London Dungeon**
Tube station:	London Bridge
Line(s):	______________________
	______________________
	______________________
	______________________

Sight:	**London Eye**
Tube station:	Waterloo
Line(s):	______________________
	______________________
	______________________
	______________________

b Use your short notes from a) and write short dialogues in your exercise book. Make complete sentences. The following example might help you.

Example: A: Excuse me, how do I get to Big Ben, please?
B: You are at Oxford Circus. Big Ben is near Westminster tube station. Take the Victoria Line southbound and get off at Victoria. Then change to Circle or District Line eastbound and get off at Westminster.
A: Thank you very much. Goodbye.
B: You're welcome. Goodbye.

3 **a** Read the following dialogue with a partner. Read it several times and try to look at your partner as much as possible. Are there any props/things that could make your performance more interesting? Act out the dialogue.

A: Excuse me, how do I get to Hyde Park, please?
B: Hyde Park? That's near the Marble Arch underground station. You're at Piccadilly Circus. Take the Bakerloo Line northbound to Oxford Circus. There you change to the Central Line westbound and get off at Marble Arch.
A: Well, thank you very much.
B: You're welcome. Is there anything special today? Sometimes they have great concerts there.
A: Yes. I'm going to see "The Who".
B: Oh, great. Have fun.
A: Thanks and goodbye.
B: Goodbye.

b Compare this dialogue with your dialogues from 2b. What is different? Underline the sentences which include extra information and write them down. Can you think of more possible questions or sentences for a short, friendly talk? Write them in your exercise book.

4 Choose a dialogue from 2b and add more questions and friendly phrases. Practice the dialogue and act it out.

Methode

In Gruppen bearbeiten die Schüler unterschiedliche Aufgaben. Anschließend erstellt jede Gruppe zu ihrem Thema eine Mindmap, die auf dem Tisch ausgelegt wird. Jeder Schüler innerhalb der Gruppe erhält eine Nummer. Ein Gruppenmitglied bleibt an seinem Tisch. Die anderen Schüler verteilen sich so auf die Tische, dass alle, die die gleiche Nummer erhalten haben, vor der gleichen Mindmap stehen. Der „Experte", der am jeweiligen Thema gearbeitet hat, fasst nun für seine Mitschüler die wichtigsten Informationen zusammen. Diese machen sich Notizen.
Nach einem Signal des Lehrers wechseln alle Gruppen an einen neuen Tisch und der Schüler, der an der Erstellung des nächsten Produktes beteiligt war, erklärt dieses usw. Die Exhibition ist beendet, wenn alle Filme vorgestellt wurden.

Hinweise/Tipps

Die Schüler werden in fünf Gruppen aufgeteilt und bearbeiten gemeinsam innerhalb ihrer Gruppe jeweils einen Text über einen Film.
Nach dem Lesen des Textes soll in jeder Gruppe ein Austausch stattfinden, um sicherzustellen, dass der Text von allen Gruppenmitgliedern verstanden wurde. Erst danach soll jeder Schüler die wichtigsten Informationen anhand von Stichpunkten festhalten. Anschließend erstellen sie gemeinsam eine Mindmap zu dem jeweiligen Film.
Der Lehrer hat während der Exhibition zweimal die Möglichkeit, Einfluss auf die Gruppenzusammenstellungen zu nehmen. Ob Zufallsgruppen oder leistungsdifferenzierte Gruppen besser geeignet sind, sollte je nach Klasse entschieden werden. Es bietet sich jedoch gerade in der ersten Austauschphase, in der das Textverständnis und das Notieren von Stichpunkten im Vordergrund stehen, an, schwächeren Schülern eine Orientierung an leistungsstärkeren Schülern zu ermöglichen.
Alternativ können die Produkte für die zweite Austauschphase auch an unterschiedliche Wandseiten gehängt werden und die Präsentationen finden im Stehen statt.
Je nachdem, wie viel Zeit zur Verfügung steht, bietet es sich nach der Exhibition an, dass die Schüler wieder in ihre Stammgruppe zurückkehren und ihre Aufzeichnungen der unterschiedlichen Präsentationen vergleichen.
Andere Möglichkeiten, das Text- und Hörverständnis sicherzustellen, wären ein Quiz, bei dem der Lehrer Fragen zu den verschiedenen Filmen stellt, oder ein Lückentext.
Die Schüler können sich hierbei durch Fragen bei der jeweiligen Expertengruppe nochmals rückversichern.

Material

- Materialseiten 1 bis 6: je ein Text pro Gruppenmitglied
- Materialseite 7 in Klassenstärke
- bunte Stifte
- eventuell Bilder der Filme

1 GROUP A

a Read the text and mark the most important information.
b Talk to your group and discuss what you've marked.
c Take notes.
d Design a mind map with your group about the film.

Tributes of Panem

"The Tributes of Panem" is a series of three adventure novels written by the American author Suzanne Collins. The main characters are Katniss Everdeen and Peeta Mellark.
The titles are "The Hunger Games", "Catching Fire" and "Mockingjay". The film "Mockingjay" is split into two parts.

Film summary:
Panem is a country which is separated (= *aufgeteilt*) into twelve poor districts (= *Bezirke*) (formerly 13). The head of the country is the wealthy (= *reich*) Capitol, which is located in the Rocky Mountains and reigns (= *herrschen über*) the twelve districts. Every year, children between the ages of 12 and 18 are chosen to take part in a fight to the death called "The Hunger Games". The film takes place in a future time.
Katniss Everdeen lives in District 12, the poorest region, where many people die because they have nothing to eat. As punishment (= *Strafe*) for a past rebellion one boy and one girl from each district, between the ages of 12 and 18, are selected (= *ausgewählt*) by lottery to be in the Hunger Games. In the Hunger Games there only can be one winner, all the others have to kill each other.
Katniss Everdeen and Peeta Mellark from District 12 are the survivors (= *Überlebende*) of the 74th Games. They decide to commit suicide (= *Selbstmord begehen*) because they don't want to fight till there is only one winner. So the Capitol decides that there are two winners.
"Catching Fire" begins six months after the last Hunger Games. During the 75th Games a rebellion in the districts starts. Katniss is rescued (= *gerettet*) by the rebel forces (= *Streitkräfte*) from District 13.
In "Mockingjay" Peeta has been kidnapped and brainwashed (= *einer Gehirnwäsche unterzogen*) by the Capitol. Katniss is sent home to District 12, Katniss's mother and Gale both take jobs in different districts.
At the end Katniss and Peeta remain together, Peeta's love won.

Notes:

____

____

____

____

1 GROUP B

a Read the text and mark the most important information.

b Talk to your group and discuss what you've marked.

c Take notes.

d Design a mind map with your group about the film.

Twilight

"Twilight" is the first film in The Twilight Saga film series and is about the relationship between the human (= *menschlich*) girl Bella Swan (played by Kristen Stewart) and Edward Cullen, who is a 108 years old modern vampire (played by Robert Pattinson).

Film summary:
17-year-old Isabella "Bella" Swan moves to Forks, a small town near the Washington coast, to live with her father after her parents got divorced.
At her new high school, Bella sits next to Edward Cullen in biology class on her first day of school. First, Bella thinks that Edward doesn't like her and she is confused (= *irritiert*). Then she finds out that Edward is a vampire, but he only drinks animal blood. He has the ability to read minds (= *Gedanken lesen*), with the exception of (= *mit Ausnahme von*) Bella's. Edward and Bella fall in love and Edward introduces Bella to his family. Edward and his family risk their lives to protect her from evil (= *böse*) vampires.

Twilight was released (= *erschien*) on November 21, 2008. "New Moon" and "Eclipse", the next two novels in the series, were produced as films the following year.

Notes:

1 GROUP C

a Read the text and mark the most important information.
b Talk to your group and discuss what you've marked.
c Take notes.
d Design a mind map with your group about the film.

Harry Potter

"Harry Potter" is a film series based on the Harry Potter novels by author J. K. Rowling and consists of (= *bestehen aus*) eight fantasy films beginning with "Harry Potter and the Philosopher's Stone" (2001) and ending with "Harry Potter and the Deathly Hallows – Part 2" (2011). "Harry Potter and the Deathly Hallows" is split into two films. The series stars (= *in einer Hauptrolle zeigen*) Daniel Radcliffe as Harry Potter, Rupert Grint as Ron Weasley and Emma Watson as Hermione Granger.

Film summary:
Harry Potter is an orphan (= *Waise*) who lives with his uncle, aunt and cousin. They don't like him and treat (= *behandeln*) him really meanly (= *gemein*). One example: he has to sleep in a little storeroom under the stairs. At the age of eleven he finds out that he is a wizard (= *Zauberer*) who lives within the ordinary (= *gewöhnlich*) world of non-magical people, known as Muggles. The wizarding world is secret from the Muggle world because the wizards are afraid that the Muggles would hunt them down. Harry becomes a student at Hogwarts School of Witchcraft and Wizardry and it's there where most of the events in the series take place. As Harry develops through his adolescence (= *Jugend*), he learns to overcome the problems that face him: magical, social and emotional, including ordinary teenage challenges (= *Herausforderungen*) such as friendships, love and exams, and the greater test of preparing himself for the confrontation that lies ahead: facing (= *entgegentreten*) the evil (= *böse*) most powerful wizard Lord Voldemort who killed his parents.

Notes:

1 GROUP D

a Read the text and mark the most important information.

b Talk to your group and discuss what you've marked.

c Take notes.

d Design a mind map with your group about the film.

Bend it like Beckham

The film "Bend it like Beckham" was released (= *erschien*) in 2002 and is a British romantic sports and comedy-drama family film starring Keira Knightley.
Its title refers to (= *sich beziehen auf*) the football player David Beckham, who could score by „bending" the ball past a wall of defenders (= *Abwehrspieler*).

Film summary:
The movie is about the 18-year-old girl Jesminder Bhamra (nickname: Jess). She lives in London and her family has got Indian roots. Her parents have forbidden her to play football because she's a girl. She joins a local women's team, which makes its way to the top of the league.
Joe, the coach of the team, is impressed (= *beeindruckt*) by her play and puts her on the team. Jess pretends (= *vortäuschen*) to have a job to play with the team and Jules and Jess become best friends although both are attracted to (= *sich angezogen fühlen von*) Joe. Jess tells her sister Pinky the truth (= *Wahrheit*) to cover for (= *decken*) her when the team travels to Germany for a big match. Joe encourages (= *ermutigen*) Jess to tell her parents the truth and says that she has a chance to win a scholarship (= *Stipendium*), but her father doesn't believe it. Jess and Jules must sort their differences, make peace with their parents and overcome cultural prejudices (= *Vorurteile*) to win the league championship and earn scholarships to Santa Clara University in California.

Notes:

1 GROUP E

a Read the text and mark the most important information.

b Talk to your group and discuss what you've marked.

c Take notes.

d Design a mind map with your group about the film.

High School Musical

"High School Musical" is a Walt Disney production and an American teen comedy musical television film. The first part was released (= *erschien*) in 2006 and is the first series in the High School Musical trilogy. "High School Musical 2" was released in 2007 and the film "High School Musical 3" in 2008. The film's soundtrack was the best-selling album in the United States for 2006.

Film summary:
"High School Musical" is a story about two teenagers, Troy and Gabriella, who met at a karaoke contest during a winter holiday.
After the holidays, Gabriella's mother gets a new job and therefore they have to move to another city. Gabriella has to attend (= *besuchen*) a new school. At the new school, Gabriella meets Troy again, but seeing each other is not as easy as during holidays: Troy Bolton (played by Zac Efron) is the captain of the basketball team and very cool and popular at school. Gabriella (played by Vanessa Hudgens), the new student at school, is very shy (= *schüchtern*) and very good at Mathematics and Science.
They take part in a school musical casting and win. Troy's basketball team mates (= *Mannschaftskameraden*) and High school diva Sharpay Evans (played by Ashley Tisdale) will do anything to sabotage the friendship between Troy and Gabriella.

Notes:

1 GROUP F

a Read the text and mark the most important information.
b Talk to your group and discuss what you've marked.
c Take notes.
d Design a mind map with your group about the film.

Pirates of the Caribbean

"Pirates of the Caribbean" is a series of fantasy films based on Walt Disney's theme park ride (= *Themenfahrt im Freizeitpark*).
The stories follow the adventures of Captain Jack Sparrow (Johnny Depp), Will Turner (Orlando Bloom) and Elizabeth Swann (Keira Knightley).

Film summary:
The film series started in 2003 with "Pirates of the Caribbean: The Curse of the Black Pearl". The film was very successful and grossed (= *spielte ein*) US $ 654 million worldwide.
Before its release (= *Erscheinen*), many journalists had expected (= *erwarten*) the film to flop as the pirate genre had not been successful for years, but Johnny Depp's portrayal of the pirate Jack Sparrow made the film a big success.
It is a tale of adventure (= *Abenteuergeschichte*) set during the 17th century in the Caribbean Sea.
Captain Barbossa steals Captain Sparrow's ship, the Black Pearl, and kidnapps the Governor's beautiful daughter, Elizabeth Swann. There is a curse (= *Fluch*) that has doomed (= *verdammen*) Barbossa and his crew to live forever. The curse can be broken only if a previously (= *zuvor*) plundered treasure (= *Schatz*) is given back.

Notes:

2 Your teacher will give you a number. Form a group with all the pupils that have got the same number. One member of another group will present his/her film. Use this table to take notes.

Checklist

name of the film	release	actors	further information	short summary

Methode

In Gruppen bearbeiten die Schüler unterschiedliche Aufgaben. Anschließend erstellt jede Gruppe zu ihrem Thema eine Mindmap, die auf dem Tisch ausgelegt wird. Jeder Schüler innerhalb der Gruppe erhält eine Nummer. Ein Gruppenmitglied bleibt an seinem Tisch. Die anderen Schüler verteilen sich so auf die Tische, dass alle, die die gleiche Nummer erhalten haben, vor der gleichen Mindmap stehen. Der „Experte", der am jeweiligen Thema gearbeitet hat, fasst nun für seine Mitschüler die wichtigsten Informationen zusammen. Diese machen sich Notizen.
Nach einem Signal des Lehrers wechseln alle Gruppen an einen neuen Tisch und der Schüler, der an der Erstellung des nächsten Produktes beteiligt war, erklärt dieses usw. Die Exhibition ist beendet, wenn alle Filmstars vorgestellt wurden.

Hinweise/Tipps

Die Schüler werden in fünf Gruppen aufgeteilt und bearbeiten gemeinsam innerhalb einer Gruppe jeweils einen Text über einen Filmstar.
Nach dem Lesen des Textes soll in jeder Gruppe ein Austausch stattfinden, um sicherzustellen, dass der Text von allen Gruppenmitgliedern verstanden wurde. Erst danach soll jeder Schüler die wichtigsten Informationen anhand von Stichpunkten festhalten. Anschließend erstellen sie gemeinsam eine Mindmap zu dem jeweiligen Filmstar.
Der Lehrer hat während der Exhibition zweimal die Möglichkeit, Einfluss auf die Gruppenzusammenstellungen zu nehmen. Ob Zufallsgruppen oder leistungsdifferenzierte Gruppen besser geeignet sind, sollte je nach Klasse entschieden werden. Es bietet sich jedoch gerade in der ersten Austauschphase, in der das Textverständnis und das Notieren von Stichpunkten im Vordergrund stehen, an, schwächeren Schülern eine Orientierung an leistungsstärkeren Schülern zu ermöglichen.
Alternativ können die Produkte für die zweite Austauschphase auch an unterschiedliche Wandseiten gehängt werden und die Präsentationen finden im Stehen statt.
Je nachdem, wie viel Zeit zur Verfügung steht, bietet es sich nach der Exhibition an, dass die Schüler wieder in ihre Stammgruppe zurückkehren und ihre Aufzeichnungen der unterschiedlichen Präsentationen vergleichen.
Andere Möglichkeiten, das Text- und Hörverständnis sicherzustellen, wären ein Quiz, bei dem der Lehrer Fragen zu den verschiedenen Filmstars stellt, oder ein Lückentext.
Die Schüler können sich hierbei durch Fragen bei der jeweiligen Expertengruppe nochmals rückversichern.

Material

- Materialseiten 1 bis 6: je ein Text pro Gruppenmitglied
- Materialseite 7 in Klassenstärke
- bunte Stifte
- eventuell Bilder der Schauspieler

1 GROUP A

a Read the text and mark the most important information.
b Talk to your group and discuss what you've marked.
c Take notes.
d Design a mind map with your group about the actress.

Jennifer Lawrence

The American actress Jennifer Shrader Lawrence was born on August 15th, 1990. Her first big role was in the sitcom "The Bill Engvall Show" (2007–09). She also played in the dramas "The Burning Plain" (2008) and "Winter's Bone" (2010), for which she received (= *erhielt*) a nomination for the Academy Award for Best Actress. Her first international success came with the superhero film X-Men "First Class" in the year 2011.
Lawrence got international fame (= *Ruhm*) for playing the heroine (= *Heldin*) Katniss Everdeen in the "Hunger Games" film series (2012–15).

Jennifer Lawrence was born and grew up in Louisville, which is located in the US state of Kentucky. She has two older brothers, Ben and Blaine. By the age of 14, she had decided to start a career as an actress, so she persuaded (= *überredete*) her parents to take her to New York City to find a talent agent.

Jennifer Lawrence is in a position of influence (= *Einfluss*) and power within the film industry. In 2013, she was among the Time 100, a list of the most influential people in the world, published by Time Magazine. Forbes Magazine named her the second-highest-paid actress in Hollywood behind Sandra Bullock. She is named as the "most desirable (= *begehrenswert*) woman" of 2013. She is one of the highest-paid actresses of 2015, with earnings of $ 52 million.

Notes:

____

1 GROUP B

- **a** Read the text and mark the most important information.
- **b** Talk to your group and discuss what you've marked.
- **c** Take notes.
- **d** Design a mind map with your group about the actress.

Kristen Stewart

The American actress Kristen Jaymes Stewart was born on April 9th, 1990. Everybody knows her as Bella Swan in "The Twilight Saga" film series from 2008–12. She is also the "face" of the Chanel and Balenciaga fashion brands (= *Modemarken*).
Stewart began her career in 1999 and became famous by playing Jodie Foster's daughter in the 2002 thriller "Panic Room". Stewart was listed as the highest-earning (= *bestverdienend*) female actress in the Vanity Fair "Hollywood Top Earners List of 2010", with estimated earnings (= *geschätztes Einkommen*) of $ 28.5 million.

Kristen Stewart was born in Los Angeles in the US state of California, where she was raised (= *großgezogen*) by parents who worked in the entertainment industry. Her father, John Stewart, is a stage manager and television producer who has worked for Fox. Her mother, Jules Mann, has directed (= *Regie führen bei*) films. Kristen Stewart has an older brother, Cameron B. Stewart, and two adopted brothers, Dana and Taylor. As she grew up, Kristen Stewart thought she would become a director, but never considered (= *in Erwägung ziehen*) being an actress. However, she began acting at the age of eight. Her first role was a small part in a Disney Channel TV-movie. After the success of "Panic Room", Stewart got a role in another thriller, "Cold Creek Manor" (2003), as the daughter of characters played by the very famous actors Dennis Quaid and Sharon Stone. After that, she was nominated again for a Young Artist Award for her performance.
At about this time in her career, she started homeschooling because of her irregular schedule.
After meeting on the set of Twilight in 2008, Stewart was in a relationship with Robert Pattinson until 2014.

Notes:

1 GROUP C

a Read the text and mark the most important information.

b Talk to your group and discuss what you've marked.

c Take notes.

d Design a mind map with your group about the actor.

Daniel Radcliffe

The English actor Daniel Jacob Radcliffe was born on 23rd July, 1989. He played the main character in the "Harry Potter" film series. He began his acting career at the age of ten with a small part in the television film "David Copperfield". One year later, he took part in the "Harry Potter" casting and won.
He had to sign (= *unterschreiben*) a contract (= *Vertrag*) to play the main role in all "Harry Potter" films and got released (= *entbunden*) after the eighth and final film in 2011.

Daniel Radcliffe was born in West London. He is the only child of Alan George Radcliffe, a literary agent, and Marcia Jeannine Gresham, a casting agent who was involved in (= *beteiligt an*) several films for the BBC. According to (= *laut*) himself, he was not very good at school. He thought school was useless and really difficult, but he achieved (= *erzielte*) A grades in the three AS-level exams that he took in 2006. Although he had good marks, he decided to take a break from education and did not go to college or university.

In an interview, Daniel Radcliffe said that some people would never be able to separate (= *trennen*) him from the character Harry Potter, but he also is "proud (= *stolz*) to be associated (= *in Verbindung gebracht werden*) with this film series forever".
He said that although he really liked to play Harry Potter, he isn't interested in doing more "Harry Potter" films.

Notes:

1 GROUP D

a Read the text and mark the most important information.

b Talk to your group and discuss what you've marked.

c Take notes.

d Design a mind map with your group about the actress.

Keira Knightley

The British actress Keira Christina Knightley was born on 26th March, 1985. She began acting as a child on television and made her film debut in 1995. She became famous in 2002 after playing in the film "Bend It Like Beckham" and achieved international fame (= *Ruhm*) in 2003 after playing Elizabeth Swann in the "Pirates of the Caribbean" film series.
Keira Knightley got nominations for the Academy Award for Best Actress and the Golden Globe Award for Best Actress for her role as Elizabeth Bennet in "Pride and Prejudice", a story by Jane Austen. Keira Knightley is the only non-American on the list of highest-paid actresses: in 2007 she earned (= *verdiente*) $ 32 million.

Keira Knightley was born in London, England. She has an older brother named Caleb. When she was a child, she played in a number of local amateur productions. At the age of six, she got an agent who found jobs for her in commercials (= *Werbespots*) and got her roles in small TV productions.
Today, Keira Knightley is the face of an Amnesty International campaign to support (= *unterstützen*) human rights (= *Menschenrechte*).

Notes:

1 GROUP E

- a Read the text and mark the most important information.
- b Talk to your group and discuss what you've marked.
- c Take notes.
- d Design a mind map with your group about the actor.

Zac Efron

The American actor and singer Zachary David Alexander Efron was born on October 18th, 1987. His nickname is Zac. He began to act in 2000 and became very popular and famous after his leading role (= *Hauptrolle*) in the Disney Channel Original Movie "High School Musical".
Since then, Zac Efron has played in many movies, for example "17 Again", "Me and Orson Welles", "Charlie St. Cloud", "New Year's Eve", "The Lucky One", "That Awkward Moment", "Neighbors" and "The Lorax".

Zac Efron was born in California and has a brother, Dylan. His father encouraged (= *ermutigte*) him to begin acting when Zac was eleven years old.
He finished High School in 2006 and wanted to study at the University of Southern California, but had to stop because of his work on film projects.
In 2002, Zac Efron had some small roles on several television series. In 2006, he played the character Troy Bolton, a popular student and captain of the basketball team, in "High School Musical". After that movie, he became a teen idol for millions of fans. He also was second on People's 2011 Most Beautiful list.
In 2013 he had some trouble with alcoholism and drugs, but he has been clean since July 2013.

Notes:

1 GROUP F

a Read the text and mark the most important information.

b Talk to your group and discuss what you've marked.

c Take notes.

d Design a mind map with your group about the actor.

Johnny Depp

Johnny Depp's full name is John Christopher Depp. He was born on June 9th, 1963 and is an American actor, producer and musician.
He has won the Golden Globe Award and Screen Actors Guild award for Best Actor.
In the 80s, Johnny Depp became a teen idol on the television series "21 Jump Street". Since then, Johnny Depp has played very interesting supporting and leading roles (= *Neben- und Hauptrollen*) in many films, for example "Platoon" (1986), "Edward Scissorhands" (1990), "Sleepy Hollow" (1999) and, of course, "Pirates of the Caribbean". He also played in the musical adventure film "Charlie and the Chocolate Factory" (2005) and in the fantasy film "Alice in Wonderland" (2010).
Johnny Depp is regarded as (= *gilt als*) one of the world's biggest movie stars. He has been nominated for major (= *wichtig*) acting awards, including (= *darunter auch*) three nominations for Academy Award for Best Actor. He won the Golden Globe Award for Best Actor.

Johnny Depp has two children with the French actress Vanessa Paradis: daughter Lily-Rose Melody Depp (born in 1999), and son John "Jack" Christopher Depp III (born in 2002).
In 2012, Johnny Depp met actress and model Amber Heard on the set of "The Rum Diary". He got divorced and married his new girlfriend on February 3rd, 2015.
Amber Heard announced their separation on 25 May, 2016 and has started divorce proceedings.

Notes:

2 Use this table to make short notes about the movie stars.

Checklist

name					
born (age)					
place of birth					
family					
most important film					
other films					
awards					
further information					

Methode

Die Schüler beschäftigen sich mit einem Partner mit den vorgegebenen Materialien zum Thema *Relative clauses.*
In dieser Phase arbeiten sie gemeinsam an Übungen und können sich bei Unklarheiten in einem geschützten Raum gegenseitig helfen. Nach der Bearbeitung ihrer Aufgaben erstellen die Paare eigene Übungen und Rätsel, die in der nächsten Phase mit einem weiteren Partnerpaar ausgetauscht werden.

Hinweise/Tipps

In der ersten Partnerarbeitsphase beschäftigen sich die Schüler intensiv mit den englischen Relativsätzen, vor allem mit den Relativpronomen.
Sie besprechen sich mit ihrem Lernpartner und tauschen Ideen für mögliche Rätsel aus, die sie selbst erstellen. Es bietet sich hierbei an, die Schüler darauf hinzuweisen, dass die von ihnen entworfenen Aufgaben anschließend von einem anderen Partnerpaar bearbeitet werden sollen. Daher sollten sie sauber und ordentlich arbeiten und eine Lösungsseite erstellen.
Entweder kann der Lehrer die Partnerkonstellationen im Vorhinein bestimmen oder ähnlich verfahren wie bei der Methode Lerntempoduett: Sobald ein Partnerpaar mit den gesamten Aufgaben fertig ist, steht es auf und positioniert sich für andere sichtbar an einer vorher abgesprochenen Stelle im Klassenraum, um zu signalisieren, dass es fertig ist. Das nächste Paar, das seine Arbeit beendet hat, holt es ab. Zu viert suchen sie sich einen freien Platz im Klassenraum und arbeiten gemeinsam weiter, indem sie ihre erstellten Rätsel austauschen, bearbeiten und anschließend besprechen.

Material

- Materialseiten 1 und 2 in Klassenstärke

Relative clauses

1 **a** Which noun can be replaced by which relative pronoun? Place them into the correct category in the list below.

DVD woman cat actor mobile phone
boy magazine remote control
customer movie tablet picture
girl music star shop Snoopy, the dog key

who	which

b Take a sheet of paper and create a similar exercise.

2 **a** Which relative pronoun fits? Complete the sentences with *who* or *which*.

1. My father would like to buy a washing machine ______________ is easy to handle.
2. Is this the dog ______________ played in "A dog named Beethoven"?
3. This is the bus ______________ has got a TV and a DVD player.
4. This is the saleswoman ______________ sold us the car.
5. Is this the actress ______________ played in the Harry Potter movie?

b Complete the sentences. Cross out the gap when you can leave out *who* or *which*.

1. Is this the picture ______________ your friend sent me?
2. Lee-Byung-Chull is one of the men ______________ founded the Samsung Group.
3. The Odysseum is an adventure museum in Cologne ______________ the whole family will love.
4. The mobile phone ______________ your friend has got is too small for me.
5. Joan K. Rowling is a writer ______________ is very famous.

c Take a sheet of paper. Create two exercises similar to 2a and b.

3 **a** Make sentences about the following famous people / film / thing.
Add *who* or *which*.

Johnny Depp
– actor
– crazy Jack Sparrow in
"Pirates of the Caribbean"

Pulp fiction
– US cult movie
– produced by Quentin
Tarantino

1. ______________________________
____
____
____

2. ______________________________
____
____
____

Elyas M'Barek
– German actor
– lives in Munich

WhatsApp
– a chat service
– send videos or photos

3. ______________________________
____
____
____

4. ______________________________
____
____
____

b Take a sheet of paper and create a similar exercise. Think of a famous person, musician, actor or company and write down some short notes about him, her or it. Make sure that a relative clause is possible.

Methode

Im Double circle begegnen die Schüler nach Ablauf eines vorher vereinbarten Zeitraums neuen Partnern zur weiteren Zusammenarbeit. Dadurch erhalten sie bei jedem Partnerwechsel neue Ideen und können im Anschluss an die Double circle-Phase entscheiden, von welchem Ausgangspunkt aus sie weiterarbeiten möchten. Somit ist auch eine sinnvolle Differenzierung gewährleistet, da auf die Kreativität und Ideenfindung verschiedener Lernpartner gleichzeitig zurückgegriffen werden kann.

Hinweise/Tipps

In der Einzelarbeitsphase beschäftigen sich die Schüler intensiv mit den Ländern, Städten und Besonderheiten des Vereinigten Königreiches.
Je nach Lerngruppe bietet sich hier alternativ auch eine Partnerarbeit an, um den Schülern vor dem Austausch mit anderen Schülern mehr Sicherheit zu geben.
Das Rotieren im Kugellager muss vor der Durchführung von der Lehrperson klar durchdacht sein: Sie muss festlegen, welcher Kreis beginnt und in welchem Kreis wie viele Personen nach rechts oder links gehen, um doppelte Gesprächspartner zu vermeiden und Bewegung ins Spiel zu bringen.
Es ist außerdem empfehlenswert, den Arbeitsauftrag mit Handbewegungen zu unterstreichen, da eine Richtungsangabe, je nachdem welcher Kreis sich angesprochen fühlt, oftmals zu Verwirrungen führt (Beispiel: Die Anweisung „The inner circle moves three persons to the right." sollte mit einer Geste in die zu laufende Richtung untermalt werden.).
Um zu überprüfen, ob das eben Gesagte verstanden wurde, empfiehlt es sich, eine Check-up-Phase einzulegen: Die Schüler, die gerade die Rolle des Zuhörers eingenommen haben, erklären einem neuen Partner der „Expertengruppe", was sie verstanden haben. Der „Experte" kann helfen, korrigieren oder zustimmen. Diese Check-up-Phase kann auch mehrmals erfolgen.
Ist der Klassenraum zu eng, kann die Double circle-Phase je nach Lerngruppe und Gegebenheiten der Schule vor dem Klassenraum durchgeführt werden.

Material

- Materialseite 1 in Klassenstärke
- Materialseiten 2 bis 4 in halber Klassenstärke
- eventuell Bilder der Länder

1 **a** Label the map and colour in the parts of the United Kingdom.

b Use a map or the Internet and fill in the capitals of the provinces and the big cities.

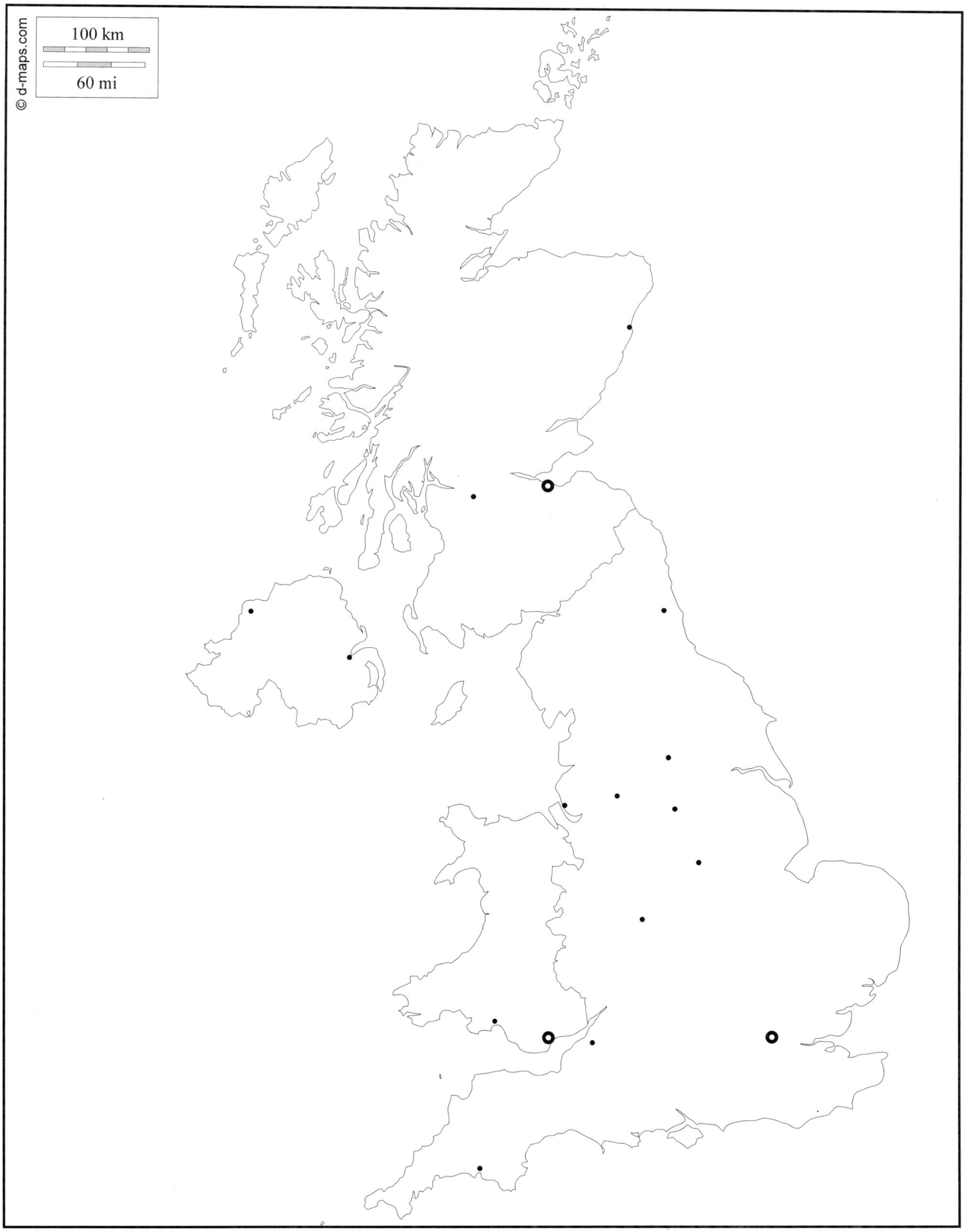

Quelle: http://d-maps.com/carte.php?num_car=11719&lang=de

2 a PARTNER A

Work with a partner. Try to fill in the boxes about the provinces of the United Kingdom.
You can use the Internet, your English book and a dictionary.

England

Capital: ____________________

Population: ____________________

Area: ____________________

Language(s): ____________________

Big cities: 1. ____________________

2. ____________________

3. ____________________

Famous sports: ____________________

____

Other interesting information:

____

____

____

Wales

Capital: ____________________

Population: ____________________

Area: ____________________

Language(s): ____________________

Big cities: 1. ____________________

2. ____________________

3. ____________________

Famous sports: ____________________

____

Other interesting information:

____

____

____

b Talk to your partner about the two provinces you've had a look at. Also listen to his/her information. Write down what you can remember; then find an expert in class and check if your notes are correct.

2 a PARTNER B

Work with a partner. Try to fill in the boxes about the provinces of the United Kingdom.
You can use the Internet, your English book and a dictionary.

Scotland

Capital: ______
Population: ______
Area: ______
Language(s): ______
Big cities: 1. ______
2. ______
3. ______
Famous sports: ______

Other interesting information:
______

Northern Ireland

Capital: ______
Population: ______
Area: ______
Language(s): ______
Big cities: 1. ______
2. ______
3. ______
Famous sports: ______

Other interesting information:
______

b Talk to your partner about the two provinces you've had a look at. Also listen to his/her information. Write down what you can remember; then find an expert in class and check if your notes are correct.

2 PARTNER A

a Read the text and mark the most important information.

b Read it again and write down short notes in your exercise book.

c Talk to a partner and tell him/her what you've learned about England.

England

England is a small country in the northwest of Europe with a huge population. More than 53 million people live there. London is not only the capital of England; it's the capital of the United Kingdom. About 8.5 million people live in this beautiful city. The most famous river of England is Thames. It's about 346 km long and connects London with the North Sea. The capital is also the residence of the Royal Family, who carry out a lot of public engagements (= *Verpflichtungen*). The head of state is Queen Elisabeth II.
The highest mountain in England is Scafell Pike, which is about 980 metres high. Unique characteristics (= *einzigartige Besonderheiten*) are the beautiful nature and the impressive (= *beeindruckend*) coasts. Sports are very popular in England – first and foremost football, cricket and rugby. Popular English celebrities (= *Berühmtheiten*) are David Beckham, Daniel Craig, Kate Winslet, Keira Knightley, Mick Jagger and Elton John.

2 PARTNER B

a Read the text and mark the most important information.

b Read it again and write down short notes in your exercise book.

c Talk to a partner and tell him/her what you've learned about Scotland.

Scotland

Scotland is in the north of Great Britain and a part of the United Kingdom. More than 5.3 million people live there; its area is about 78,500km^2 (compare: Germany's area is four times bigger).
The capital of Scotland is Edinburgh. About 450,000 people live there. Edinburgh is only the second biggest city of Scotland. The biggest city is Glasgow with a population of about 650,000 people.
In Scotland there are two official languages: English and Gaelic.
Scotland is a country with a lot of history; therefore there are a lot of interesting and beautiful sights, for example castles, ancient (= *alt*) villages and ruins. Scotland is surrounded (= *umgeben*) by 790 small islands, but only 130 of them are occupied (= *bewohnt*). The most famous islands are the Orkney Islands, the Isle of Skye and Islay. Each island has its own character and fantastic nature.
Near the coast you often find huge rocks and beautiful beaches. The head of state is Queen Elisabeth II. Famous Scottish people are Amy MacDonald, Sean Connery and Gerald Butler.

Methode

Die grundlegende Arbeitsweise bei diesem Thema ist der Dreischritt Ich – Du – Wir. Auf diese Weise erarbeiten die Schüler Themen selbstständig und erweitern ihre soziale Kompetenz, indem sie mit einem Partner gemeinsam an einem Lösungsweg arbeiten.
Think-Phase: Die Schüler machen sich eigenständig mit dem Thema vertraut, stellen Bezüge zu ihrem Vorwissen her und entwickeln erste Ideen.
Pair-Phase: Gemeinsam mit einem Partner (i. d. R. Banknachbar) folgt der Austausch über Gehörtes/Gelesenes oder Gesehenes. Gemeinsam arbeiten sie an ihren Ergebnissen/Lösungen.
Share-Phase: Die Resultate werden dem Plenum präsentiert und gegebenenfalls diskutiert.

Hinweise/Tipps

Bei dem vorgeschlagenen Dreischritt Think – Pair – Share kann eine weitere Phase zwischengeschoben werden: die Square-Phase. Diese Phase geht der Share-Phase bzw. der Präsentation im Plenum voraus. Besonders für unsichere Gruppen/Teams eignet sich diese Phase, da Schüler so die Möglichkeit haben, ihre Ergebnisse zunächst in Kleingruppen (Vierergruppen) vorzustellen, bevor sie diese vor der Klasse präsentieren.
Hierbei kann der Lehrer die Partnerkonstellationen im Vorhinein bestimmen oder so verfahren: Sobald ein Partnerpaar mit den gesamten Aufgaben fertig ist, steht es auf und positioniert sich für andere sichtbar an einer vorher abgesprochenen Stelle im Klassenraum, um zu signalisieren, dass es fertig ist. Das nächste Paar, das seine Arbeit beendet hat, holt es ab. Zu viert suchen sie sich einen freien Platz im Klassenraum und arbeiten gemeinsam weiter.

Material

- Materialseiten 1 bis 3 in Klassenstärke

1 a Write down the correct English sentences using the *will*-future.

3rd pers. pl.	*nicht im Park spazieren*
3rd pers. sg.	*im See schwimmen*
2nd pers. pl.	*Freunde treffen*
1st pers. sg.	*nicht ein Museum besuchen*
1st pers. pl.	*die Pferde füttern*
2nd pers. sg.	*nicht ins Kino gehen*

1. ______________________________
2. ______________________________
3. ______________________________
4. ______________________________
5. ______________________________
6. ______________________________

b Read the answers and write down the matching question in *will*-future.

1. ______________________________?

– No, we won't visit Uncle Theo this weekend.

2. ______________________________?

– Yes, we'll be at the concert at 7.30.

3. ______________________________?

– No, I won't go shopping at the weekend.

4. ______________________________?

– Yes, our neighbour will buy a new horse.

5. ______________________________?

– No, my friends won't take the tram.

c Negate the following sentences correctly. Use the *will*-future.

1. Justin and Kevin ______________ (*essen*) in a restaurant.
2. We ______________ (*gehen*) for a walk.
3. My grandparents ______________ (*genießen*) the dirty air in the city.
4. My aunt ______________ (*machen*) breakfast.
5. I ______________ (*schreiben*) a postcard.
6. She ______________ (*gehen*) to riding lessons.

d What will be in 20 years? Ask the fortuneteller. Write down questions using the *will*-future.

Will I be married?

Will I be rich?

2 Work with a partner. Use your questions from exercise 1d. One of you is the fortuneteller and the other one is the customer. The fortuneteller has to think of possible answers to the questions. The customer writes short notes. Then take turns. (For the fast ones: find another fortuneteller in your class.)

question	fortune teller 1	fortune teller 2
Will I be married?		
Will I be rich?		

3 **a** In a group of four think of other *will*-future questions about this afternoon, next weekend and next year. Everybody has to find at least two questions. Every group member has to write down all the questions in his/her exercise book.

b Choose a question and ask your left neighbour. He/she gives an answer and continues in a clockwise direction.

c You know the German game "Ich packe meinen Koffer". Talk about what you will do tomorrow. Repeat every sentence of your group members.
Who can remember the most sentences?

Example:
Paul: I'll play football tomorrow.
Tim: Paul will play football and I'll go to the cinema tomorrow.
Nadja: Paul will play football, Tim will go to the cinema and I'll meet my friend tomorrow.
Etc.

Methode

Die grundlegende Arbeitsweise bei diesem Thema ist der Dreischritt Ich – Du – Wir. Auf diese Weise erarbeiten die Schüler Themen selbstständig und erweitern ihre soziale Kompetenz, indem sie mit einem Partner gemeinsam an einem Lösungsweg arbeiten.
Think-Phase: Die Schüler machen sich eigenständig mit dem Thema vertraut, stellen Bezüge zu ihrem Vorwissen her und entwickeln erste Ideen.
Pair-Phase: Gemeinsam mit einem Partner (i. d. R. Banknachbar) folgt der Austausch über Gehörtes/Gelesenes oder Gesehenes. Gemeinsam arbeiten sie an ihren Ergebnissen/Lösungen.
Share-Phase: Die Resultate werden dem Plenum präsentiert und gegebenenfalls diskutiert.

Hinweise/Tipps

Bei dem vorgeschlagenen Dreischritt Think – Pair – Share kann eine weitere Phase zwischengeschoben werden: die Square-Phase. Diese Phase geht der Share-Phase bzw. der Präsentation im Plenum voraus. Besonders für unsichere Gruppen/Teams eignet sich diese Phase, da Schüler so die Möglichkeit haben, ihre Ergebnisse zunächst in Kleingruppen (Vierergruppen) vorzustellen, bevor sie diese vor der Klasse präsentieren.
Hierbei kann der Lehrer die Partnerkonstellationen im Vorhinein bestimmen oder so verfahren: Sobald ein Partnerpaar mit den gesamten Aufgaben fertig ist, steht es auf und positioniert sich für andere sichtbar an einer vorher abgesprochenen Stelle im Klassensaal, um zu signalisieren, dass es fertig ist. Das nächste Paar, das seine Arbeit beendet hat, holt es ab. Zu viert suchen sie sich einen freien Platz im Klassenraum und arbeiten gemeinsam weiter.

Material

- Materialseiten 1 und 3 in Klassenstärke
- Materialseite 2 in halber Klassenstärke
- farbige Stifte
- Scheren

Conditional sentences I+II

1 **a** You are planning a weekend trip to a big city with your friends. What will you see there? Describe the picture in complete sentences. Also describe where the things are. The prepositions in the box might help you.

in the background	in the foreground	on the right	on the left
at the bottom	on top	on	under
in the middle	between	next to	near
in front of	behind		

b What will you and your friends do at the weekend? Write five sentences in your exercise book.

2 **a** Say what you and your friends will do on your weekend trip. Complete the sentences and be careful with the tense.
Colour the main clause red, the subordinate clause green. Then label which sentence is a conditional I and which one a conditional II.

If the weather is rainy at the weekend, ______________________________. ☐

If it's sunny at the weekend, ______________________________. ☐

If we got tickets, ______________________________. ☐

We'll go to the tourist information if ______________________________. ☐

If my best friend went with us, ______________________________. ☐

If we get lost, ______________________________. ☐

I'd book a room in an expensive hotel if ______________________________. ☐

I'll send you a postcard if ______________________________. ☐

We wouldn't take the train if ______________________________. ☐

b Can you think of other possible *if*-clauses about the weekend trip? Write five sentences in your exercise book.

3 **a** Cut out the 20 cards and divide them between you and your partner. One partner starts by laying a card on the table. The other one tries to find a matching phrase. Then take turns.

WE WILL HAVE FUN IF	MY MOTHER WOULDN'T BE HAPPY	IF PAUL SEES A SPIDER
THE WEATHER IS NICE	IF I GOT LOST IN THE FOREST	I WOULD BE SO SAD
MY PARENTS WOULD BUY A HORSE	HE WILL CATCH IT	I WOULD FEED THE HORSES EVERY DAY
DON'T GIVE IT MILK	IF THEY HAD A FARM	IF HE SEES OUR MOTHER ON A HORSE
IF MY CAT DIED	IF WE HAD A FARM	If I NEED HIM
IF HER HUSBAND DIDN'T WORK IN THE CITY	IF YOU FIND A BABY HEDGEHOG	KELLY WOULD MOVE TO THE COUNTRY
MY BROTHER WILL LAUGH	MY BEST FRIEND WILL HELP ME	

b Write the matching pairs in your exercise book. Watch the spelling and the punctuation.

c Work with your partner and make your own cards with *if*-clauses. First write the sentences on an extra sheet of paper and check them carefully. Then write the main sentences and the *if*-clauses with capital letters in separate boxes and cut them out. You will need the cards for the next group work. Don't forget to write the solution on an extra sheet of paper.

4 Form groups of at least four members. Use the cards you've made and play the *if*-clause game. Use the following rules:

- Eyerybody gets five cards which should lie in front of each player facing the sentences.
- Put the rest of the cards on a pile and turn over the first card.
- The youngest player starts the game by finding a matching phrase. If a sentence is possible, he/she takes the pair and gets a point. If no sentence is possible, he has to take a new card from the pile.
- The player on the left continues.
- The player with the highest score wins the game.

Rules clear? Ready, steady, go!

Methode

Die Schüler beschäftigen sich anhand der vorbereiteten Materialien auf zwei verschiedene Arten mit Rollenspielen: Sie entwickeln einen Dialog anhand genauer Vorgaben und sie erarbeiten ein Gespräch und eine Präsentation nur auf Basis einer vorgegebenen Idee.
Das Rollenspiel bietet sich bei diesem Thema an, da die Schüler in Partner- und Gruppenarbeit in unterschiedliche Rollen schlüpfen und so auf spielerische Art und Weise Dialogstrukturen einüben können. Da die Materialien zum großen Teil in Partner- und Gruppenarbeit zu bearbeiten sind, werden die Lernenden in ihrer kommunikativen und sozialen Kompetenz gefördert.

Hinweise/Tipps

Die Schüler beschäftigen sich mit den vorgegebenen Materialien zum Thema *Meeting friends*.
Je nach Bedarf können die Aufgaben allein oder mit einem Partner erledigt werden. Bei einer Partnerarbeit haben gerade schwächere Schüler die Möglichkeit, sich bei Unklarheiten in einem geschützten Raum gegenseitig zu helfen. Die Schüler wiederholen zunächst gemeinsam Wortschatz und Fragestrukturen, um sich über Hobbys, Freizeitaktivitäten und Orte in der englischen Sprache zu unterhalten. Anhand von Bildimpulsen sollen sie sich an einen Ort und in eine Freizeitaktivität hineinversetzen und ein Gespräch erfinden, welches möglicherweise in dieser Situation stattfinden könnte. Gemeinsam gestalten die Schüler einen Dialog und üben diesen ein. Er wird anschließend vor der Klasse oder einem anderen Partnerpaar präsentiert.
Es ist empfehlenswert, die Schüler auf mögliche Requisiten hinzuweisen. Durch Requisiten fällt es vielen Schülern leichter, in eine andere Rolle zu schlüpfen bzw. eine erfundene Situation darzustellen.

Material

- Materialseiten 1 bis 3 in Klassenstärke
- eigene Requisiten für die Dialoge

1 **a** Create a wanted poster of yourself. You can also add a photo.

First name: ____________________

Middle name: ____________________

Last name: ____________________

Nickname: ____________________

Date of birth: ____________________

Place of birth: ____________________

That's me!

Address: ____________________

Telephone number: ____________________

Size: ____________________

Eye colour: ____________________

Favourite colour: ____________________

Favourite food: ____________________

Favourite star: ____________________

Favourite subject: ____________________

Hobbies: ____________________

Dream job: ____________________

I like: ____________________

I don't like: ____________________

Special about me: ____________________

b Which words are new for you? Look them up in a dictionary. Write them in your exercise book and translate them into German.

c Use the short notes from the wanted poster and write a text about yourself. Write it in your exercise book.

2 **a** Before you talk to a partner, prepare some questions that you want to ask him/her. Write them in your exercise book. The questions in the box might help you.

- How are you?
- What did you do yesterday?
- What will you do today?
- Where do you live?
- How old are you?
- Did you like it?
- Do you have a pet?
- What is your favourite food?
- Which music do you like?
- Do you like your class?
- What is your telephone number?
- Do you play football?
- Have you seen the new film with Elyas M'Barek?
- Who is your form teacher?
- Who is your favourite sports star?
- Who is your form teacher?
- What is your favourite ice-cream?

b Talk to a partner. Start and finish your talk in a friendly way. Take turns in asking questions. Try to stay in the English language. Talk to your partner for at least five minutes.

c After talking try to remember some of your partner's answers and write them down in your exercise book.

3 **a** Where can you meet your friends? Write down some places in the boxes below.

Meeting friends

b Now add activities you can do with your friends at these places.

4 **a** Look at the pictures with a partner and write down some words/thoughts/short notes that occur to you. If you don't know the words, look them up in a dictionary.

1. 

2. 

3. 

4. 

5. 

6. 

b Choose a picture with your partner and write a dialogue in your exercise book. Who are the kids in the picture? What are their names? What are they talking about? What do they want to do? It sometimes helps to ask and answer some questions before you start to write.

c Practise the dialogue and act it out. Can you think of any props (= *Requisiten*) that might make your performance more interesting or funnier?

d Find another couple and create a role play with four persons.

Methode

Beim Speeddating begegnen die Schüler nach Ablauf eines vorher vereinbarten Zeitraums neuen Partnern zur weiteren Zusammenarbeit. Sie sitzen ihrem Gesprächspartner an einer Tischreihe gegenüber und rücken auf ein Signal hin einen Platz weiter. Dadurch erhalten sie bei jedem Partnerwechsel neue Ideen. Während der Speeddating-Phase können die Schüler den Dialog in einem geschützten Raum vortragen.

Hinweise/Tipps

In der Einzelarbeitsphase beschäftigen sich die Schüler intensiv mit Fragestrukturen und Redemitteln zum Thema Sport. Alternativ könnte man hier auch eine Partnerarbeit hinzuziehen, um den Schülern vor dem Speeddating einen Austausch über die Aufgaben zu ermöglichen.
Für das Speeddating eignen sich je nach Lerngruppengröße ca. zehn Tische in einer Reihe.
Es empfiehlt sich, die Tischreihen erst zu stellen, nachdem die Einzelarbeitsphase (bzw. Partnerarbeit) beendet wurde.
Entweder kann der Lehrer die Gruppenkonstellationen (wer sitzt auf der A- oder B-Seite?) bestimmen oder die Schüler setzen sich nach dem Zufallsprinzip gegenüber. Durch das rotierende System ergeben sich immer individuelle Gesprächskonstellationen. Um den Überblick zu behalten, ist es von Vorteil, eine Schülerseite (z. B. A) sitzen zu lassen und nur die andere Schülerseite aufzufordern, einen Platz weiter zu rutschen. Je nach Lerngruppe und Zeitbudget kann das Speeddating beliebig oft durchgeführt werden. Es empfiehlt sich (wie auf der Checkliste vorgegeben), den Dialog mindestens viermal sprechen zu lassen. Als akustisches Signal zum Unterbrechen der Gespräche eignet sich eine Tischglocke, eine Rassel oder ein anderes den Schülern bekanntes Geräusch.

Material

- Materialseiten 1 bis 3 in Klassenstärke
- eventuell Bilder einer Lieblingssportart
- Tischglocke, Rassel o. Ä.

All about sports

1 Create an acrostic with words that have something to do with sports: sport categories, sports equipment, sports locations etc.

A
L
L

A
B
O
U
T

S
P
O
R
T
S

2 **a** Where do you do it and what do you need?

sport	location	equipment
dancing		
basketball		
skiing		
riding		
swimming		
canoeing		
football		
volleyball		

b Make a list and match the verbs to the nouns: *(to) play, (to) go, (to) do.*
Translate the nouns into English and write them in the correct column.

1. Judo
2. Volleyball
3. Schwimmen
4. Tischtennis
5. Kanufahren
6. Basketball
7. Surfen
8. Reiten

(to) play	(to) go	(to) do

3 Create this mind map about your favourite sport. You can also use photos or pictures from magazines.

Where?

When?

My favourite sport

What? (equipment)

Who?

How?

Why?

4 **a** Work together with a partner. Write down the name of your speed dating partner and ask him/her questions about his/her favourite sport. Interview seven classmates and write down short notes about their answers.

your partner's name	favourite sport	Where?	When?	What? (equipment)	Who?	Why?

b Choose four classmates that you have interviewed and write about their favourite sports activities. Write complete sentences in your exercise book.

Wenn keine Lösungen angegeben wurden, handelt es sich um offene, individuelle Lösungen.

Seite 6:

1 a

Beispiellösung:

BUCKINGHAM PA**L**ACE
T**O**WER BRIDGE
BRICKLA**N**E
TROCA**D**ERO
L**O**NDON EYE
NATURAL HISTORY MUSEUM

PICCADILLY CIRCU**S**
LONDON BR**I**DGE
GHERKIN
HOUSES OF PARLIAMENT
MADAME **T**USSAUDS
WE**S**TMINSTER ABBEY

1 b

TOWER BRIDGE, TROCADERO, BRICK LANE
GHERKIN, MADAME TUSSAUDS, PICCADILLY CIRCUS

Seite 14:

1 a

a	b	c	d	e	f	g	h	i	j	k	l	m	n	o	p	q	r	s	t	u	v	w	x	y	z
15	10	2	4	6	12	9	8	1	14	5	16	17	3	7	11	13	23	22	25	26	18	19	20	21	24

Seite 15:

2 a

1. What's your name?
2. How old are you?
3. How tall are you?
4. What is your address?
5. Where are you from?
6. Who is your favourite actor?
7. What are your hobbies?
8. What is your hair colour?
9. What is your eye colour?
10. What do you like?
11. What don't you like?
12. What is special about you? / What are you good at?

Seite 16:

3 a

Beispiellösungen:
Who is Paul?
Why does Paul live in that house?
What is behind the green house? / What is Paul's favourite food?
When did Paul move in?
Where is the house? / Where does Paul go to school?

3 b

Beispiellösungen:
Is Paul good at school?
Does Paul play tennis?
Has Paul got a brother?

4 a

Beispiellösung:
A: Excuse me, can you help me, please?
B: Yes, of course. How can I help you?
A: I'm lost. I'm looking for the youth hostel.
B: The youth hostel is not far. Turn right at the next traffic lights. You can't miss it.
A: Thank you very much.
B: You're welcome. Have a nice day.
A: I wish you a nice day, too.

Seite 18:

1 a

underground lines	stations	verbs	other words (adjectives, nouns ...)
Bakerloo	Piccadilly Circus	get on	southbound
Central	Chancery Lane	change to	Travelcard
Circle	Moorgate	get off	northbound
District	Temple		westbound
Hammersmith & City	Queensway		rush hour
Jubilee	Paddington		zone
Metropolitan	Temple		eastbound
Northern	Victoria		platform
Piccadilly	Angel		
Waterloo & City			
Victoria			

Seite 19:

2 a

Sight: **Buckingham Palace**
Tube station: St. James's Park
Line(s): Victoria Line southbound
get off at Victoria
change to Circle or District Line eastbound
get off at St. James's Park

Sight: **The Trocadero**
Tube station: Piccadilly Circus
Line(s): Bakerloo Line southbound
get off at Piccadilly Circus
(only one stop)

Sight: **Natural History Museum**
Tube station: South Kensington
Line(s): Victoria Line southbound
get off at Green Park
change to Piccadilly Line westbound to South Kensington

Sight: **Madame Tussauds**
Tube station: Baker Street
Line(s): Bakerloo Line northbound
get off at Baker Street
(only two stops)

Seite 20:

Sight: **The London Dungeon**
Tube station: London Bridge
Line(s): Central Line eastbound
get off at Bank
change to Northern Line northbound
get off at London Bridge

Sight: **London Eye**
Tube station: Waterloo
Line(s): Bakerloo Line northbound
get off at Waterloo

2 b

Buckingham Palace
A: Excuse me, how do I get to Buckingham Palace, please?
B: You are at Oxford Circus. The Buckingham Palace is near the Tube station St. James's Park. Take the Victoria Line southbound and get off at Victoria. Then change to the Circle or District Line eastbound and get off at St. James's Park.
A: Thank you very much. Goodbye.
B: You're welcome. Goodbye.

The Trocadero
A: Excuse me, how do I get to the Trocadero, please?
B: You are at Oxford Circus. The Trocadero is near the Tube station Piccadilly Circus. Take the Bakerloo Line southbound and get off at Piccadilly Circus. There's one stop only.
A: Thank you very much. Goodbye.
B: You're welcome. Goodbye.

Natural History Museum
A: Excuse me, how do I get to the Natural History Museum, please?
B: You are at Oxford Circus. The Natural History Museum is near the Tube station South Kensington. Take the Victoria Line southbound and get off at Green Park. Then change to the Piccadilly Line westbound to South Kensington.
A: Thank you very much. Goodbye.
B: You're welcome. Goodbye.

Madame Tussauds
A: Excuse me, how do I get to Madame Tussauds, please?
B: You are at Oxford Circus. Madame Tussauds is near the Tube station Baker Street. Take the Bakerloo Line northbound and get off at Baker Street. There are two stops only.
A: Thank you very much. Goodbye.
B: You're welcome. Goodbye.

The London Dungeon
A: Excuse me, how do I get to the London Dungeon, please?
B: You are at Oxford Circus. The London Dungeon is near the Tube station London Bridge. Take the Central Line eastbound and get off at Bank. Then change to the Northern Line northbound to London Bridge.
A: Thank you very much. Goodbye.
B: You're welcome. Goodbye.

London Eye
A: Excuse me, how do I get to the London Eye, please?
B: You are at Oxford Circus. The London Eye is near the Tube station Waterloo. Take the Bakerloo Line northbound and get off at Waterloo.
A: Thank you very much. Goodbye.
B: You're welcome. Goodbye.

3 b

– Is there anything special today? Sometimes they have great concerts there.
– Yes. I'm going to see "The Who".
– Oh, great. Have fun.

Seite: 38

1 a

who	which
woman	DVD
actor	cat
boy	mobile phone
customer	magazine
girl	remote control
music star	movie
Snoopy, the dog	tablet
	picture
	shop
	key

2 a

1. My father would like to buy a washing machine <u>which</u> is easy to handle.
2. Is this the dog <u>who</u> played in "A dog named Beethoven"? (*who* bei Tieren mit Namen)
3. This is the bus <u>which</u> has got a TV and a DVD player.
4. This is the saleswoman <u>who</u> sold us the car.
5. Is this the actress <u>who</u> played in the Harry Potter movie?

2 b

1. Is this the picture <u>(/)</u> your friend sent me?
2. Lee-Byung-Chull is one of the men <u>who</u> founded the Samsung Group.
3. The Odysseum is an adventure museum in Cologne <u>(/)</u> the whole family will love.
4. The mobile <u>(/)</u> your friend has got is too small for me.
5. Joan K. Rowling is a writer <u>who</u> is very famous.

Seite 39:

3 **a**

1. Johnny Depp is an actor who plays the crazy Jack Sparrow in "Pirates of the Caribbean".
2. Pulp fiction is a US cult movie which was produced by Quentin Tarantino.
3. Elyas M'Barek is a German actor who lives in Munich.
4. WhatsApp is a chat service which you use to send videos or photos.

Seite 41:

1 **a** + **b**

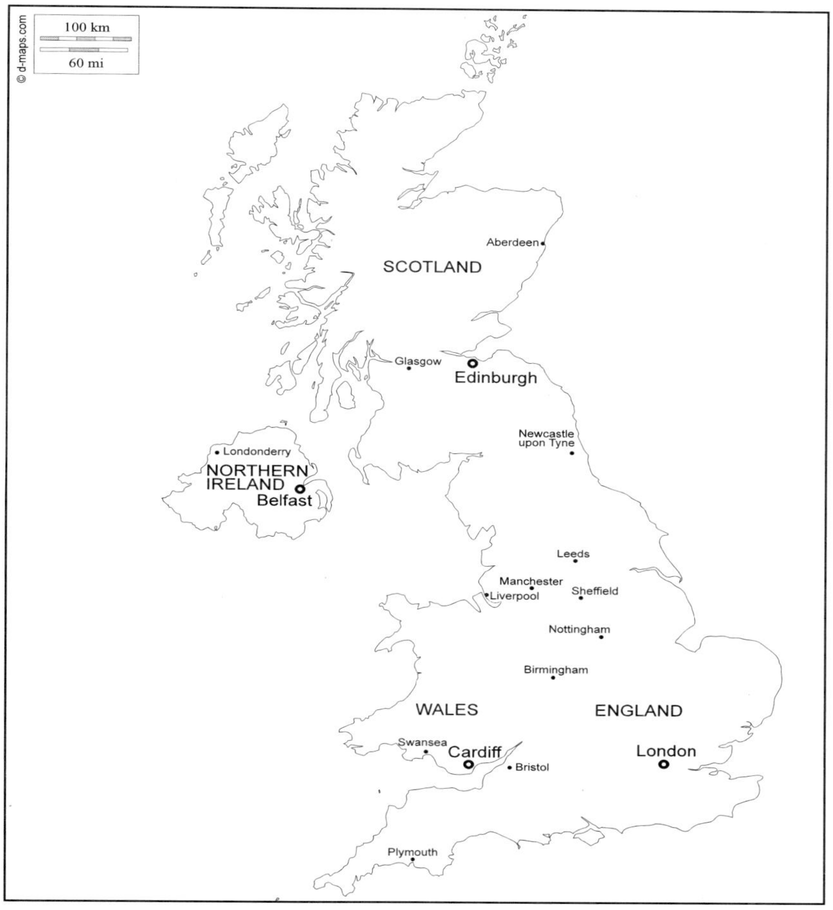

Seite 42:

2 **a**

PARTNER A

England	
Capital:	London
Population:	54,310,000 people
Area:	130,395 km²
Language(s):	English
Big cities:	1. London 2. Birmingham 3. Manchester
Famous sports:	football, cricket, tennis
Other interesting information:	British Royal family

Wales	
Capital:	Cardiff
Population:	3,092,000 people
Area:	20,761 km^2
Language(s):	English and Welsh
Big cities:	1. Cardiff 2. Swansea 3. Newport
Famous sports:	rugby, football, snooker
Other interesting information:	Duffy and Catherine Zeta-Jones are Welsh celebrities.

Seite 43:
PARTNER B

Scotland	
Capital:	Edinburgh
Population:	5,347,600 people
Area:	77,910 km^2
Language(s):	English and Gaelic
Big cities:	1.Glasgow 2. Edinburgh 3. Aberdeen
Famous sports:	Highland Games (contest), football, golf
Other interesting information:	famous national treasures: whisky, kilt and bagpipe

Northern Ireland	
Capital:	Belfast
Population:	1,840,500 people
Area:	13,843 km^2
Language(s):	English and Irish
Big cities:	1. Belfast 2. Londonderry 3. Lisburn
Famous sports:	(Gaelic) football, cricket, rugby
Other interesting information:	Northern Ireland conflict (the Troubles)

Seite 46:

1 a

1. They won't go for a walk in the park.
2. He/She/It will go swimming in the lake.
3. You will meet friends.
4. I won't visit a museum.
5. We will feed the horses.
6. You won't go to the cinema.

1 b

1. Will you/we visit Uncle Theo this weekend?
2. Will you/we be at the concert at 7.30?
3. Will you go shopping at the weekend?
4. Will your/our neighbour buy a new horse?
5. Will your friends take the tram?

1 c

1. Justin and Kevin won't eat in a restaurant.
2. We won't go for a walk.
3. My grandparents won't enjoy the dirty air in the city.
4. My aunt won't make breakfast.
5. I won't write a postcard.
6. She won't go to riding lessons.

Seite 50:

1 a

Beispiellösung:
On the right there's a car park. On the left, opposite the car park, a man is leaving a bank. Two people are sitting on a fountain, which is in the middle of the picture. One of them has got a dog. Many cars and buses are passing the fountain. In the foreground there's a taxi. Behind the fountain some people are climbing the steps. They're going past a department store and walking towards a big hotel in the background of the picture.

2 a

Beispiellösung:

main clause / subordinate clause	
If the weather is rainy at the weekend, **we'll visit a lot of museums**.	I
If it's sunny at the weekend, **we'll do a lot of sightseeing**.	I
If we got tickets, **we would see the musical**.	II
We'll go to the tourist information if we need help.	I
If my best friend went with us, **we would have a lot of fun**.	II
If we get lost, **we'll ask for the way**.	I
I'd book a room in an expensive hotel if I had a lot of money.	II
I'll send you a postcard if I've got time.	I
We wouldn't take the train if it wasn't the fastest way to get there.	II

Seite 51:

3 a

Mögliche Lösungen:
We will have fun if the weather is nice.
My mother wouldn't be happy if I got lost in the forest.
If Paul sees a spider, he will catch it.
My parents would buy a horse if they had a farm.
I would be so sad if my cat died.
I would feed the horses every day if we had a farm.
If you find a baby hedgehog, don't give it milk.
If he sees our mother on a horse, my brother will laugh.
My best friend will help me if I need him.
Kelly would move to the country if her husband didn't work in the city.

Seite 55:

3 **a** + **b**

Beispiellösung:

at the ice cream parlour: eat ice cream, chat, watch other people
at the swimming pool: go swimming, play beach volleyball, play table tennis
in the park: go jogging, play football, have a picnic
at home: listen to music, chat, play computer games
at the sports field: play ball games, do sports
in the city: go shopping

Seite 56:

4 **a**

Beispiellösung:

1. swimming pool, jump, play, fun, sunny weather, cold water, friends, happy, laugh, …
2. ice cream, strawberry, sunny, friend, talk, city, enjoy, taste, meet friends, laugh, …
3. sports, skateboard, longboard, halfpipe, free time activity, hobby, dangerous, accident, fun, fast, …
4. enjoy, relax, book, read, exciting, story, quiet, friend, free time activity, …
5. watch DVD, friend, crisps, funny, laugh, exciting, stay up late, talk, …
6. computer game, fun, exciting, meet friends, battle, …

Seite 58:

1

Beispiellösung:

ST**A**DIUM
VO**L**LEYBALL
SKI S**L**OPE

PL**A**Y
BAT
JUD**O**
TENNIS CO**U**RT
IN-LINE SKA**T**ES

RUNNING **S**HOES
BRIDLE **P**ATH
CAN**O**E
RACKET
LEO**T**ARD
SWIMMING TRUNK**S**

2 **a**

sport	location	equipment
dancing	gym/sports hall	leotard, dancing shoes, music
basketball	gym/sports hall/playground	basketball, shoes, shorts, basket
skiing	ski slope	skies, helmet
riding	bridle path/field/beach	helmet, saddle
swimming	swimming pool	swimsuit, swimming trunks
canoeing	river/lake	canoe, life-jacket
football	pitch/sports field/park	football boots, football
volleyball	gym/sports hall/beach	volleyball, net

Seite 59:

2 b

(to) play	(to) go	(to) do
volleyball	swimming	judo
table tennis	canoeing	
basketball	surfing	
	riding	

3

Beispiellösung:

My favourite sport:	football
Where?	on the pitch
When?	every Tuesday evening
What?	football boots, football
Who?	my best friends and I
How?	I play well.
Why?	I see my friends/It's fun.

Double circle

Ziele

- Eine Anwendungssituation für Informationen wird geschaffen.
- Die Verankerung der Inhalte im Gedächtnis wird gefördert.
- Das aktive Sprechen und das aktive Zuhören werden geübt.
- Die Schüler trainieren die Fähigkeit, die wichtigsten Inhalte zusammenzufassen und zu strukturieren.

Voraussetzungen

- Die Schüler sollten sich gegenseitig zuhören können.
- Die Schüler sollten erste Kompetenzen im Vermitteln von Wissensinhalten besitzen.

Vorgehensweise

Es handelt sich um eine spezielle Form der Partnerübung. Die Schüler bilden mit ihren Stühlen einen Innenkreis und einen Außenkreis. Die Schüler aus dem Außenkreis sitzen einem Schüler aus dem Innenkreis (siehe Skizze) gegenüber. Die Schülerpaare erhalten einen kommunikativen Auftrag. Einer erzählt, der andere hört zu. Nach ca. drei Minuten (abhängig vom Lerninhalt) bewegen sich die Schüler im Innenkreis oder im Außenkreis eine Position nach links oder rechts weiter (die Richtung vorgeben!). Dadurch entstehen immer neue Partnerkombinationen.

Veranschaulichung

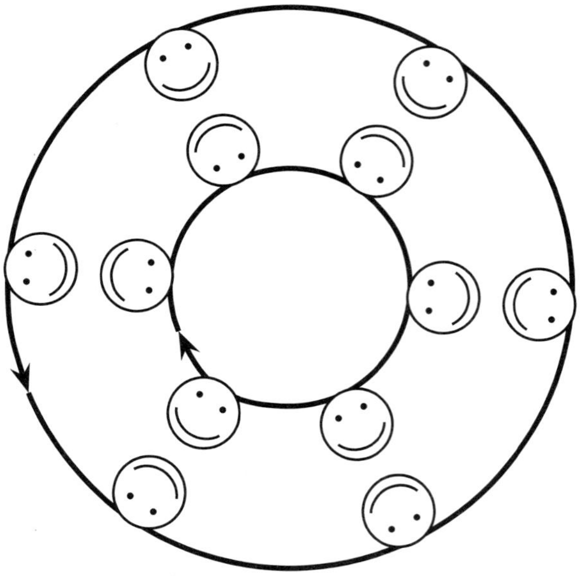

Hinweise/Tipps zur Durchführung

- Der Klassenraum sollte die notwendige Größe aufweisen.
  Alternativ kann die Methode auch in Form des „Eckenwanderns“ durchgeführt werden (d. h. statt dem Kreis werden die vier Ecken des Raumes genutzt).
- Gerade, wenn die Methode neu eingeführt wird, sollte der zu erklärende Wissensinhalt nicht zu komplex sein.
- Die Zeit von fünf bis zehn Minuten pro Durchgang sollte nicht überschritten werden.
- Um die Nachhaltigkeit und die Zuhörbereitschaft der Schüler zu vergrößern, könnte das erworbene Wissen in einer nachfolgenden Sicherungsphase entsprechend gefestigt bzw. auch abgefragt werden.

Exhibition (Ausstellung)

Ziele

- Die Schüler erklären sich gegenseitig unterschiedliche Lerninhalte und werden so zu Experten ihres Themas.
- Sie übernehmen Verantwortung und lernen durch lehren.
- Sowohl genaues Zuhören als auch eigenständiges Vermitteln werden geschult.
- Soziale Kompetenzen werden gestärkt.
- Die Organisations- und Strukturierungsfähigkeit der Schüler wird gefördert.
- Die Schüler üben sich im Präsentieren.

Voraussetzungen

- Die Schüler können einander aufmerksam zuhören.
- Sie sind in der Lage, sich stichpunktartig Notizen zu machen.
- Der Klassenraum bietet ausreichend Platz.
- Die Schüler können Lernplakate strukturiert gestalten.

Vorgehensweise

Während der Vorbereitungsphase erarbeiten die Schüler zu dritt oder zu viert ein Unterrichtsthema und gestalten dazu ein Lernplakat mit den wichtigsten Inhalten. In der sich anschließenden Ausstellungsphase werden die Lernplakate so im Klassenraum platziert, dass genügend Platz zwischen ihnen ist. Ein Gruppenmitglied bleibt bei dem Lernplakat der Gruppe. Alle anderen gehen durch den Klassenraum und lassen sich an den Plakaten der anderen Gruppen über die fremden Unterrichtsinhalte informieren. Sie notieren dabei die wichtigsten Aspekte stichpunktartig. In der Informationsphase kommen die Schüler wieder in ihren ursprünglichen Gruppen zusammen und informieren die Mitschüler mithilfe ihrer Notizen über das Gehörte/Gesehene.

Hinweise/Tipps zur Durchführung

- Die Anfertigung von inhaltlich und strukturell gelungenen Lernplakaten kann sehr zeitintensiv sein. Investieren Sie unbedingt ausreichend Zeit in die sorgfältige Ausgestaltung, denn je ungenauer während dieser Phase gearbeitet wird, desto geringer ist am Ende der Lernerfolg der Klasse insgesamt.
- Lassen Sie frühzeitig zum jeweiligen Thema Bilder mitbringen, die für das Lernplakat genutzt werden können, oder stellen Sie selbst eine kleine Auswahl zur Verfügung. In diesem Fall sollten aber nicht nur Bilder zur Verfügung stehen, die unbedingt auf das Lernplakat sollen. Auch die Diskussion über die Bildauswahl innerhalb der Gruppe bedeutet einen Lernerfolg und Kompetenzzuwachs.
- Entweder sollten die Schüler bereits mit bewusster Layoutgestaltung vertraut sein oder aber mithilfe dieser Methode und einer anschließenden Reflexion darin geschult werden.
- Legen Sie klare Regeln fest, wie viele Personen sich vor einem Plakat aufhalten dürfen, damit vermieden wird, dass sich alle an einer Stelle tummeln, während andere Gruppen nicht zum Präsentieren ihrer Ergebnisse kommen.
- Planen Sie eine Möglichkeit ein, den Lernzuwachs zu sichern und zu überprüfen, z. B. einen Fragebogen zu allen ausgestellten Themen (auch und besonders an die „Nicht-Experten").

Partner teaching

Ziele

- Mehrere Perspektiven und Lösungsmöglichkeiten werden im Tandem besprochen.
- Die Schüler helfen sich, je nach gebildetem Tandem, gegenseitig, was eine sinnvolle Differenzierung ermöglicht.
- Die Motivation der Schüler wird gefördert.
- Die Schüler werden im Argumentieren und Kommunizieren geschult. Es entstehen Redeanlässe.
- Eigenständiges Arbeiten im Austausch mit Gleichaltrigen wird gefördert.
- Die Partnerarbeit bildet eine wichtige Vorstufe zur Teamfähigkeit und damit für die Gruppenarbeit.

Voraussetzungen

- Die Schüler sollten sozial in der Lage sein, mit einem anderen Lernpartner zusammenzuarbeiten und mit diesem in den Dialog zu treten.
- Die Schüler sollten es gewöhnt sein, selbstverantwortlich und selbstständig zu arbeiten.

Vorgehensweise

Das Tandemprinzip ermöglicht das Bilden arbeitsfähiger Zweierteams. Zwei Schüler erledigen eine Aufgabe gemeinsam, selbstständig und kooperativ.

Hinweise/Tipps zur Durchführung

- Die Zusammenstellung der Partner kann, je nach Zielsetzung, nach unterschiedlichen Kriterien erfolgen:
  - Bilden annähernd leistungshomogener Paare: Hier ist die Differenzierung durch die Wahl der Aufgabenstellung bzw. durch Hinweise/Tipps möglich. Eine arbeitsteilige Partnerarbeit kann an dieser Stelle sinnvoll sein.
  - Bilden leistungsheterogener Paare: Je nach Stärke des einzelnen Partners können dessen Fähigkeiten zur Kompensation von Schwächen des Gegenübers genutzt werden. Partnerarbeit findet in diesen Fällen meistens in arbeitsgleicher Form statt.
  - Bilden von Tandems nach Sitzordnung (d. h. mit dem Tischnachbarn): Diese Wahl hat den Vorteil, dass sie sich organisatorisch gut umsetzen lässt (keine Unruhe durch Platzwechsel). Weiterhin wird dadurch gewährleistet, dass beide Lernpartner sozial verträglich zusammenarbeiten.
- Findet ein Schüler, z. B. aufgrund seiner Außenseiterposition, keinen Partner, muss der Lehrer steuernd eingreifen. An dieser Stelle können z. B. Schüler mit hohen sozialen Fähigkeiten als Lernpartner bestimmt bzw. angesprochen werden.
- Achten Sie darauf, dass die Partner einander zugewendet arbeiten. Sonst besteht die Gefahr, dass es sich um keine Partnerarbeit, sondern um zwei Einzelarbeiten handelt.

Role play

Ziele

- Dem Schüler werden fremde Perspektiven deutlich (Steigerung der Empathiefähigkeit). Die Schüler handeln dabei nur in ihrer Rolle, d. h. auch Konfliktsituationen werden im „geschützten Raum“ dargestellt.
- Die Methode übt auch in Konfliktsituationen den friedlichen Umgang miteinander.
- Experimentierfreude, Kreativität und Lust am Sprechen werden gefördert, ebenso Flexibilität, Kommunikationsfähigkeit und Offenheit.
- Das Rollenspiel ist der szenischen Interpretation sehr ähnlich. Während bei der szenischen Interpretation jedoch das Textverständnis das eigentliche Ziel ist, wird das Rollenspiel genutzt, um Situationen „im straffreien Raum“ auszuprobieren.
- Soziale Kompetenzen werden dadurch geschult.

Voraussetzungen

- Die Schüler sollten die Bereitschaft besitzen, sich auf ein Rollenspiel einzulassen (wird mit zunehmendem Alter schwieriger).
- Die Ernsthaftigkeit der Methode wird von den Schülern wahrgenommen.

Vorgehensweise

Die Schüler „schlüpfen in die Haut“ einer anderen Person und gestalten in spielerischer Art und Weise eine vom Lehrer vorgegebene Situation vor der Klasse. Die Rolle kann konkret vorgegeben oder von den Schülern eigenständig mit Inhalt gefüllt werden.
Die Methode besteht aus folgenden Phasen:

- Vorbereitungsphase
  Die Schüler müssen sich mit der einzunehmenden Rolle bzw. mit den verschiedenen Positionen beschäftigt haben.

- Das eigentliche Spiel
  Zwei oder mehr Schüler stellen die vorher festgelegten Positionen bzw. Personen dar. Gegebenenfalls sind für die Zuschauer geeignete Beobachtungsaufgaben festzulegen.

- Abschlussbesprechung
  Verschiedene Fragestellungen sollten ausgetauscht werden (Was hat dir gefallen? Wie glaubwürdig wurden die Rollen dargestellt? Was ist dir inhaltlich aufgefallen? Gibt es Verbesserungsvorschläge? ...).

Hinweise/Tipps zur Durchführung

- Wichtig ist, die genaue Spieldauer festzulegen (nicht zu lange, da sonst kontraproduktiv).
- Sollte ein Rollenspiel in eine nicht intendierte Richtung verlaufen, muss die Lehrkraft gegebenenfalls regulierend eingreifen.
- Der jeweilige Schüler muss vor der Abschlussbesprechung wieder aus seiner Rolle herausgeholt werden. Jetzt spricht jeder Schüler wieder für seine Person und nicht für die vorher dargestellte.

Speed dating

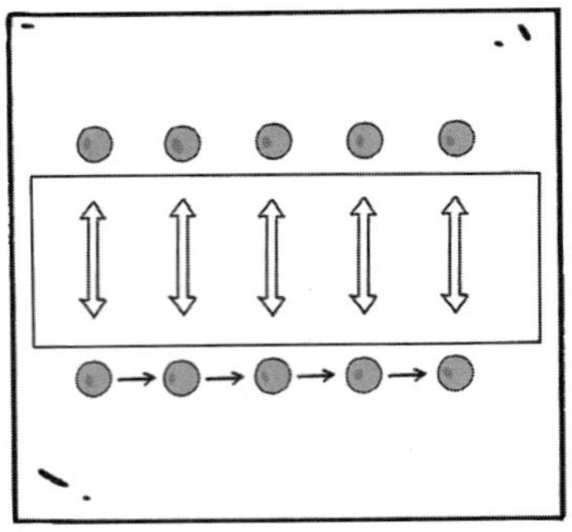

Ziele
- Eine Gesprächssituation wird geschaffen.
- Die Verankerung der Inhalte im Gedächtnis wird gefördert.
- Das aktive Sprechen und das aktive Zuhören werden geübt.
- Die Schüler trainieren die Fähigkeit, die wichtigsten Inhalte zusammenzufassen und zu strukturieren.

Voraussetzungen
- Die Schüler sollten sich gegenseitig zuhören können.
- Die Schüler sollten erste Kompetenzen im Vermitteln von Wissensinhalten besitzen.

Vorgehensweise

Es handelt sich um eine spezielle Form der Partnerübung. Die Schüler bilden mit ihren Tischen eine lange Tafel und sitzen sich jeweils partnerweise gegenüber. Die Schülerpaare erhalten einen kommunikativen Auftrag, wobei der Lehrer bestimmt, welche Seite zu sprechen anfängt. Nach ca. drei Minuten (abhängig vom Lerninhalt) wird die eine Seite aufgefordert, einen Platz nach links oder rechts (die Richtung vorgeben!) weiter zu rutschen. Dabei steht der Schüler am Tischende auf und nimmt an der vorderen Tischseite wieder Platz. Dadurch entstehen immer neue Partnerkombinationen. Wichtig hierbei ist, dass die eine Schülerseite komplett sitzen bleibt.

Hinweise/Tipps zur Durchführung
- Der Klassenraum sollte die notwendige Größe aufweisen.
- Gerade, wenn die Methode neu eingeführt wird, sollte der zu erklärende Wissensinhalt nicht zu komplex sein.
- Die Zeit von fünf bis zehn Minuten pro Durchgang sollte nicht überschritten werden.
- Um die Nachhaltigkeit und die Zuhörbereitschaft der Schüler zu vergrößern, könnte das erworbene Wissen in einer nachfolgenden Sicherungsphase entsprechend gefestigt bzw. auch abgefragt werden.

Think – Pair – Share (Ich – Du – Wir)

Ziele

- Der Anteil echter Lernzeit wird erhöht.
- Die Schüler können sich Inhalte eigenständig erarbeiten und diese vertiefen. Eigene Ideen, Lösungsmöglichkeiten und unterschiedliche Perspektiven treffen aufeinander und werden gemeinsam weiterentwickelt.
- Die Schüler erhalten die Möglichkeit, eigene Schwierigkeiten zu erkennen und mit anderen zu beheben.
- Allgemeine soziale Kompetenzen und wichtige Schlüsselqualifikationen für das bevorstehende Berufsleben werden aufgebaut, z. B. Teamfähigkeit und Rücksichtnahme.
- Die Schüler werden durch die Redeanlässe im Argumentieren und Kommunizieren geschult.
- Die Schüler helfen sich gegenseitig und schaffen so eine sinnvolle Differenzierung.

Voraussetzungen

Die Schüler sollten sozial in der Lage sein, mit anderen in Gruppen zusammenzuarbeiten und mit diesen in Dialog zu treten. Vorteilhaft wäre hier, wenn die Lernenden die Methode der Gruppenarbeit bereits anwenden können.

Vorgehensweise

Die Methode wird in drei Phasen durchlaufen:

1. Think (Ich): Individuelles Arbeiten
   Die Schüler machen sich eigenständig mit der Themenstellung vertraut. Sie stellen individuelle Bezüge zu ihrem Vorwissen her, entwickeln erste Ideen und erproben eigene Lösungsstrategien. Gleichzeitig identifizieren sie persönliche Lücken und Hemmnisse.
2. Pair (Du): Austausch mit dem Partner
   Die Schüler tauschen sich mit einem Partner (z. B. Banknachbar) aus. Dabei wechseln die Rollen zwischen Informant und Zuhörer. Die Partner fragen bei Bedarf nach, helfen sich gegenseitig bei der Klärung offener Fragen und diskutieren strittige Punkte. Gemeinsam arbeiten sie an der Optimierung des Lösungsweges.
3. Share (Wir): Austausch in der Gruppe
   Die Partnergruppen gleichen ihre Ergebnisse in einer Gruppenarbeit (vier bis sechs Personen) ab und einigen sich auf eine gemeinsame Präsentation.

Veranschaulichung

Hinweise/Tipps zur Durchführung

Zur Konzeption der Lerntandems und der Lerngruppe gibt es verschiedene Möglichkeiten:

1. Jeder Schüler sucht sich selbstständig nach der Ich-Phase seinen Partner für die Du-Phase. Weiterhin können sich die Schüler auch selbstständig für die Gruppenphase (Wir-Phase) organisieren. Eine Größe von drei bis fünf Schülern wäre hier sinnvoll. Die Praxis hat gezeigt, dass es hilfreich ist, wenn die Lehrkraft auf jeden Fall eine konkrete Anzahl vorgibt.
2. Die Lehrkraft bestimmt den jeweiligen Lernpartner (Du-Phase) und die konkrete Gruppenzusammensetzung in der Wir-Phase.

Bildquellenverzeichnis

S. 7: Tower Bridge © Oleksandr Tkachenko – Fotolia.com
Buckingham Palace © Oleksandr Tkachenko – Fotolia.com

S. 8: Madame Tussauds © Christian Schütt – Wikipedia.org (CC-by-sa 3.0/de)
Brick Lane Market © Aqwis – Wikipedia.org (Attribution ShareAlike 3.0; leicht verändert)

S. 9: London Eye © slouankang – Fotolia.com
Hyde Park © David Hawgood – Wikipedia.org

S. 10: London Dungeon © www.CGPGrey.com – Wikipedia.org
The Trocadero © Mark Hillary – Wikipedia.org

S. 11: Natural History Museum © Zachi Evenor – Wikipedia.org
Piccadilly Circus © Luciano Mortula – Shutterstock.com

S. 41: Karte United Kingdom © d-maps:
http://d-maps.com/carte.php?num_car=11719&lang=de (leicht verändert)

S. 44: Themse © samott – Fotolia.com
Schottland © MEV-Verlag

S. 65: Karte United Kingdom © d-maps:
http://d-maps.com/carte.php?num_car=18153&lang=de (leicht verändert)